A Civilization of Love

A
Civilization
OF
LOVE

*What Every Catholic Can Do to
Transform the World*

CARL ANDERSON

HarperOne
An Imprint of HarperCollinsPublishers

HarperOne

A CIVILIZATION OF LOVE: *What Every Catholic Can Do to Transform the World*. Copyright © 2008 by Carl Anderson. All rights reserved. Printed in the United States of America. No part of this book may be used or reproduced in any manner whatsoever without written permission except in the case of brief quotations embodied in critical articles and reviews. For information address HarperCollins Publishers, 10 East 53rd Street, New York, NY 10022.

HarperCollins books may be purchased for educational, business, or sales promotional use. For information please write: Special Markets Department, HarperCollins Publishers, 10 East 53rd Street, New York, NY 10022.

HarperCollins Web site: http://www.harpercollins.com
HarperCollins®, ⬛®, and HarperOne™ are
trademarks of HarperCollins Publishers

FIRST EDITION

Designed by Level C

The Library of Congress Cataloging-in-Publication Data is available upon request.

ISBN 978-0-06-133531-0

08 09 10 11 12 RRD(H) 10 9 8 7 6 5 4 3 2 1

For Dorian *always*

I invite you to carefully study the social doctrine of the Church so that its principles may inspire and guide your action in the world. May the Holy Spirit make you creative in charity, persevering in your commitments, and brave in your initiatives, so that you will be able to offer your contribution to the building up of the "civilization of love." The horizon of love is truly boundless: it is the whole world!

—*Pope Benedict XVI*[1]

Contents

Introduction

Lieutenant Daniel O'Callaghan was one of the heroes who sacrificed his life for freedom on September 11, 2001. His body was identified, in part, by the Knights of Columbus rosary that was found clutched in his hand. Like so many of his colleagues, Lieutenant O'Callaghan walked into the World Trade Center Tower on September 11, 2001, and as he did so, he walked into the hearts of a generation of Americans. I never met Danny O', but months after his death, I met and spoke about him with members of his family. I have thought about him often since.

In the days immediately following the terrorist attack on the Twin Towers and the Pentagon, when American flags seemed to be flying everywhere and we could not sing "America the Beautiful" without tears coming to our eyes, we had a precious moment as a nation to ask how we could move forward in a way that not only kept faith with but built upon the legacy of the men and women who gave their lives on September 11.

Since then, another question—what the historian Samuel Huntington calls an issue of identity—has also made its presence felt.[1] It echoes remarks made by British prime minister Sir Winston Churchill, when he addressed a joint session of the U.S. Congress within weeks of the Japanese attack on Pearl Harbor. After recounting the story of that attack and the subsequent aggressions against the British, Filipino, and American peoples elsewhere in the Pacific—acts that Churchill described as "outrages"—he went on to ask, "What kind of a people do they think we are?"[2] The atrocities committed on September 11 have caused many Americans to ask Churchill's question again: "What kind of a people do they think we are?" As the wars continue in Afghanistan and Iraq, that question continues to echo with a pressing urgency. Perhaps more important, we should ask, "What kind of a people do *we* think we are?" And what kind of a people are we *becoming?*

These questions have grown ever more pressing in the dawning years of the third millennium. Many of us—especially those who watched the inauguration of President John F. Kennedy and heard him promise that Americans would "bear any burden"[3] in the cause of freedom—had come to believe that our struggle for freedom ended with the dismantling of the Iron Curtain and the collapse of the Soviet Union. In the early 1990s, Francis Fukuyama even proclaimed "the end of history" because of this triumph of liberal democracy.[4] Now we know that the struggle of which Kennedy spoke extends further along the horizon of history than we had thought. Huntington has spoken of "the clash of civilizations," pitting Western democracy against the Islamic world. Huntington has also portrayed the threat to the United States as lying in biculturalism at home. "In the late twentieth century," he writes, "developments occurred that, if continued, could change America into a culturally bifurcated Anglo-Hispanic society with two national languages."[5] The danger is all the more alarming, Huntington says, because our national values and liberties are rooted in an Anglo-Protestant culture that is now rapidly becoming the bailiwick of a minority.[6]

Up to a point, Huntington is right. There is an increasing bicultural rift that has been made more acute by the continuing national debate over immigration. But I would like to suggest that the more fundamental cultural rift is different from what Huntington describes. It is not a division between Anglo and Hispanic, English and Spanish, North and South, Protestant and Catholic. While these cleavages cannot be ignored, they are far less central than another divide that cuts across all these categories and splits society much more deeply, in part because it splits individuals more deeply. It is the division between what Pope John Paul II has called a culture of life and a culture of death.

This terminology may seem too harsh to some, even perhaps counterproductive in terms of a national debate. But John Paul II was serious about its application and used the comparison repeatedly throughout his long pontificate. He used these two polarities not to describe a particular culture but to describe cultural values between which he saw every culture moving. He understood that no culture can remain static, just as no person can remain static. On the one hand is a culture that sees human beings as having an intrinsic value that is given and confirmed by God. On the other hand is a culture that sees human beings as the products of blind, mechanical, and amoral forces, one in which human life has only a kind of quantitative, economic value. Individuals are seen as units of production (or consumption), and those who cannot prove they have value in these terms—the unborn, the elderly, the disabled—are increasingly subject to removal by procedures such as abortion and euthanasia. Although these procedures are clothed in a humanitarian guise, we can wonder how humane their consequences will prove to be.

One of the most original cultural documents of the past generation is Art Spiegelman's Pulitzer Prize–winning *Maus*, in which the author recounts his father's experiences in the Nazi death camps. *Maus* is drawn in comic-book form, portraying the Nazis as cats and the Jews as mice. At one point in the story, the Jews in the elder Spiegelman's town in Poland are ordered to assemble in a stadium. "Then was a selection," he relates, "with people sent either to the left, either to the right [*sic*]. Old people, families with lots of kids, and people without work cards [were] all going to the left! We understood that this must be very bad." So it was: "Those on the bad side never came anymore home."[7]

Those who had no quantitative value in Hitler's sinister anti-utopia were decreed to be unworthy of life.

We should be careful of invidious comparisons between the horrors of the last century and today's culture. Obviously, there are great differences of both kind and degree that must not be overlooked. At the same time, we need to remember that there is always present to every society a sort of cultural temptation—just as there is always present a temptation to every individual human heart. And just as with the individual, we must realize that as a society, we are tempted precisely because at some level we desire something because we think it is good.

The totalitarianism of the twentieth century, both fascist and communist, was based on an explicit repudiation of the Christian tradition that had guided much of our civilization up to that point. One of the most important elements of that tradition has to do with human worth. Fascism and communism valued human beings only insofar as they were useful to the state. Today we still have to ask, is the right to life to be dependent on one's economic utility, or upon being "wanted" by someone or something? Does each of us have a value that is intrinsic, or is it provisional? Can it be taken away by someone else's fiat?

These concerns may seem too abstract for many people. Yet, as Richard Weaver once wrote, "ideas have consequences."[8] The issues addressed in this book strike at us every day—in the frantic atmosphere of many workplaces, in the increasing isolation of the family from society and of family members from each other, and in a deep internal confusion in the individual that may well be the cause of so much of the anxiety and depression that we see in today's America. I would go further and say that if you have ever felt you were trapped in a soulless world, or that the world seems to be headed in the wrong direction, that the values you see in society around you are not those that you hold in your inmost heart, this book, this call to active hope, is for you.

This book is intended as part of a discussion or, if you will, a discourse that has been going on in the Catholic Church for more than forty years now. Since the Second Vatican Council of 1962–1965, the Catholic Church has challenged cultures on a global basis by a set of values inspired by its understanding of each person's true vocation. This challenge has been guided by the late Pope John Paul II, one of the greatest popes of modern times, as well as by his successor, Pope Benedict XVI. Both of these men took part in Vatican II and influenced its outcome. Now, the popes are among the best-known individuals on earth. In light of this great visibility, it is surprising how little known is the vision of these popes. Their trips are widely broadcast but chiefly as historical events or sources of general inspiration; almost never are they discussed for what they really are: the concrete and specific presentation of how we may create what John Paul II called a "civilization of love."[9]

This book is meant to fill this gap and explore the implications of this call to build a civilization of love. This, I believe, is the only approach that offers an authentic solution to the current problems of meaning and purpose in human life. It also holds out the most hope of forestalling a clash of civilizations around the globe as well as a clash among various minorities within the United States. Moreover, it is a call to a new solidarity with the poor and all those in need. And while I believe the building of a civilization of love is the responsibility of every Christian, all Christians must work to realize this vision in such a way that Jews, Muslims, and others are welcome to participate. Building a civilization of love can only proceed on the basis of a commitment to religious freedom, tolerance, and respect for every person's human dignity.

Americans are a profoundly practical people. For all our idealism, we tend to be suspicious of ideas that do not have some application in the day-to-day world. In order to help ground these ideas as fully as possible, at the end of each chapter I have made some simple and practical suggestions for implementing them in our daily lives.

As Supreme Knight of the Knights of Columbus, a fraternal organization with more than 1.7 million members worldwide, I have worked with thousands of Christian men and their families in seeking to build a civilization of love in very practical ways through volunteer service to their communities and churches. The Knights of Columbus was founded in 1882 upon the principles of charity and unity—two values essential to the work of building a civilization of love. Today, the Knights of Columbus also operates a substantial and highly rated life-insurance company for the benefit of its members and their families—I have had the opportunity to see how such values can operate successfully in the reality of the business world. These principles are not arbitrary dictates to be blindly followed; they are integral to the healthy functioning—and profitability—of any organization, just as they are to the healthy life of an individual.

The Knights of Columbus has adopted over time as a fraternal greeting among members, *Vivat Jesus!*, the Latin words for "May Jesus live!" Simply put, this book is about what those two words mean today for his disciples as they live in and seek to influence their culture. For John Paul II, the reality of Jesus—as the one who perfectly radiates the love of God—alive and present in his life carried a responsibility to build a civilization that reflects that same love to every person. Too often, Christians have allowed this responsibility to become blunted by controversies surrounding the legal issues involved in the separation of church and state. Those issues are certainly important, but they are of secondary importance for the Christian who has a responsibility to focus upon a more fundamental issue: the *unity* of Christ and culture and the implications of that unity upon the actions of his or her daily life.

Lieutenant O'Callaghan had a habit of leaving little messages for his wife and children on Post-it notes before he left in the morning to join the firefighters at Ladder Company 4. On many days he would write simply: "I love you." As a firefighter, Danny O'Callaghan was committed to saving lives. We might say that in their profession he and his colleagues had dedicated their lives to building a culture of life. I believe Danny was also helping to build a civilization of love. Each of us has that same opportunity to build a civilization of love or not. Do we have the courage to make the choice that he did? I believe that millions of us do and that millions of us already have. I hope that this book will, in some small way, bring those of us committed to this effort more closely together.

I

The Power of Christ to Transform Culture

Pope John Paul II often spoke of the Christian's responsibility living in what he called the new "Areopagus of culture."[1] The phrase recalls the apostle Paul's preaching to the citizens of Athens in the first century—one of the first great encounters of Christianity with pagan civilization. Today it is commonplace to speak of a "clash of civilizations." Several years ago, it was just as common to speak of "culture wars," and some people continue to do so. But such encounters between civilizations or cultural values are nothing new. They have happened over and over again in the course of history, in episodes that are sometimes cataclysmic, sometimes subtle, and almost unnoticed. One such moment is Paul's preaching in Athens as recorded in the Acts of the Apostles.[2] By recalling the Areopagus so often in the context of culture, I think John Paul II was suggesting to us that what St. Paul did in Athens remains an important model for every Christian in understanding the promise of Christ to transform culture.

Paul's visit took place probably sometime between A.D. 50 and 58.[3] The setting was Athens, "the school of Greece."[4] The Romans, who had ruled the city for over a hundred years, called it *doctae Athenae*, "learned Athens." For the Romans, Athens held a central place in the evolution of their culture. Here, wrote Cicero, "civilization, learning, religion ... laws and institutions are supposed to have arisen, and to have been disseminated over the whole earth."[5] If Athens was the symbolic center of civilization, the center of activity in Athens was the Areopagus, the "hill of Ares."

Today the Areopagus, a rocky outcropping in the center of Athens, is chiefly a tourist site, from which one can photograph the much more famous and imposing Acropolis or the sprawling modern city below. In the first century, however, the Areopagus was the seat of the city's council, the core of its administrative and judicial system. Just as important, it was one of the places in which the Athenians gathered to indulge the restless curiosity for which they were so renowned. "All the Athenians and the foreigners who lived there spent their time in nothing except telling or hearing something new."[6]

In his discourse, St. Paul would not disappoint the Athenians in their expectation to hear something new. But he begins disarmingly by mentioning an altar he has seen in Athens to "an unknown god." Building such an artifact was a strange act of reverence, and Paul hints at the highly ambiguous nature of classical religion by saying that the Athenians must be "very religious"[7]—a word in the Greek original that could also be translated as "very superstitious." For the Greeks, the world was teeming with gods that inhabited the sky, the earth, and, it seemed, each tree and rock and stream. As charming as this may look to us, it had a sinister aspect. Any of these countless gods could be offended, bringing ruin to a city, and it was not always easy to tell which god might have been the culprit. So the Athenians hedged their bets with an altar to an "unknown god"—some deity that might have been overlooked in the crowd.

But the God of whom Paul speaks is not some minor spirit. He is the one, transcendent God in whom "we live, and move, and have our being,"[8] and he does not dwell in temples or in statues made of silver and gold. Then Paul departs still more radically from the classical pagan mentality. He says that God has resurrected a man whom the world has killed, and it is this man who will judge the world in righteousness at the end of history, when, indeed, all the dead will be raised.

Paul's listeners hardly know what to make of his speech. Although their myths tell of a distant past in which the gods came down to earth and lived and even mated with humans, the Athenians have never heard such a claim made about a man who has lived in recent times. And while they were familiar with a full gamut of beliefs about the afterlife (including heaven, hell, and reincarnation), no one has ever proposed to them that the dead might rise again, or that God might intervene in human history and even bring it to an end. Some laugh at Paul; others put him off, saying, "We will hear you again about this."[9] Only a few believe. Scholars and theologians have debated whether St. Paul's style of preaching at the Areopagus was effective—was it a success or a failure? But what I think is more important is what Paul is saying to us about Christianity's mission in regard to culture.

Although the Areopagus hill had extraordinary influence historically in regard to pagan culture, perhaps its greatest influence was its role in *myth* as the place signifying the dependence of human law upon divine law. This role was recorded in Aeschylus's great Greek tragic play *The Eumenides* (first produced in 458 B.C.). In his drama, Aeschylus portrays the founding of the council of the Areopagus as the result of a moral contest for the establishment of an entirely new order of community justice. Orestes, who has killed his own mother in retribution for her murdering Agamemnon, her husband and his father, is haunted by the Furies, who cry out for vengeance. The goddess Athena intervenes to supplant the rule of vengeance with the rule of law, thereby transforming the institutions of classical society. At the end of the play, the dark forces of the Furies are transmuted into the Eumenides—the "kindly ones of light." Those listening to Paul proclaim a new Gospel on the site of the Areopagus would no doubt have understood the parallel he was making. They would have seen him as proclaiming a new era in which the darkness of a society that worships before "the altar of the unknown god" gives way to a new order. The Christ whom God has raised from the dead is the one who will transform their culture and their history.

The Areopagus address is one of only three speeches attributed to Paul in the Acts of the Apostles that are recounted in detail. By preaching at the Areopagus, Paul would have been understood by the early readers of Acts to be carrying the Gospel message to the very heart of classical pagan culture and its fundamental institutions. He was not preaching a message that would easily coexist with the existing pagan gods. Instead, his message proposed a fundamental transformation of that culture.

An important part of that transformation had to do with a new vision regarding human dignity and equality. By asserting that we are "God's offspring,"[10] Paul raised an additional challenge to existing pagan culture. It is true that, as Acts itself says, Paul's description of the human race as "God's offspring" comes from one of the pagan poets (scholars are not sure which one). But if this idea was implicit in the thought of classical antiquity, it was not made explicit in practice.

Although it is sometimes forgotten today, there was another, less pleasant side to Greco-Roman culture. Human dignity and equality were not taken for granted. Indeed, the opposite was true. Slavery and torture were commonplace, and even free citizens' rights were often limited and dispensable. The great Russian novelist Boris Pasternak draws a vivid picture of this contrast between the culture of the old and the culture of the "unknown God" that was to come. The ancients, he writes, "had blood and beastliness and cruelty and pockmarked Caligulas who do not suspect how untalented every enslaver is. They had the beautiful dead eternity of bronze monuments and marble columns. It was not until after the coming of Christ that time and man could breathe freely."[11]

In a way, this speech of Paul to the learned men of Athens marked the beginning of this freedom. Human dignity and equality were no longer to be mere philosophical abstractions or poetic ideals. They were to be living realities, rooted not in the arbitrary customs of men but in our common source in God: "In him we live and move and have our being."[12]

On the other hand, aside from these breaches of human dignity and equality, the classical world at the time of Paul was not a civilization that showed any obvious signs of decay. Rome ruled what was for the vast majority of its citizens the known world, and while Rome held political primacy, it had thoroughly absorbed and disseminated Greek culture and learning. As the old saying has it, "conquered Greece conquered Rome," and the two societies had merged into a whole that at that time marked the zenith of cultural, economic, military, and political power.

Today we could see ourselves in a similar position to the classical world of Paul's day. We, too, live in a civilization that can boast unprecedented triumphs in every realm of human endeavor and that seems to be at the height of its glory but that is also suffering from many injustices. We, too, live in a culture that often seems to spend its time "in nothing except telling or hearing something new." Yet, the unprecedented electronic flow of information on a global basis has blurred the continuing "newness" of Paul's message to "seek God, in the hope that they might feel after him, and find him."[13] Even so, the responsibility of Christians in our own time remains as it was in Paul's—to radically transform culture, not by imposing values from above, but through a subtler yet more powerful process—living a vocation of love in the day-to-day reality of our lives.

If a modern Paul were to choose a contemporary Areopagus, he might settle upon Davos, Switzerland, a city where over a thousand international leaders of politics, business, and intellectual life gather once a year for the World Economic Forum. Davos participants control virtually all the major international institutions, many governments, and much of the world's economic and military establishment. Several years ago, I had the opportunity to participate in this forum, where I was able to see firsthand the "Davos culture," an elite group that shares a set of values that includes internationalism, individualism, market economies, and political democracy.[14]

What would a contemporary Paul say to a gathering of the World Economic Forum? The participants would probably have little difficulty with the view of human dignity and equality that Paul might advance. But if he spoke of a God "in whom we live and move and have our being" or the death and resurrection of a man whose very existence marks the pivot point of human destiny, they might grow just as uncomfortable as Paul's original listeners. Some might question what Christianity brings to the discussion of the universal values of equality and human dignity. But for the Christian, this is precisely the point: the understanding that these values are ultimately grounded in the sacrificial love of Jesus Christ profoundly elevates them and at the same time calls out for a truly radical personal response.

In his *Message for the World Day of Peace* in 2001, John Paul II spoke of the process of globalization, which he recognized as "leading to a progressive unification of the economy, culture and society." He then said, "For the followers of the different religions are ever more conscious of the fact that a relationship with the one God, the common Father of all, cannot fail to bring about a greater sense of human brotherhood and a more fraternal life together. In God's revelation in Christ, this principle finds a radical expression: "He who does not love does not know God; for God is love.""[15]

For the Christian, the values of equality and human dignity cannot be separated from the commandment to "love one another" as Christ has loved us—the source from which equality and dignity derive their ultimate support. Toward the end of his message, John Paul II said, "The eyes of believers contemplate the image of the Crucified One. . . . Gazing upon the Crucified

One we are filled with confidence that forgiveness and reconciliation can become the normal practice of everyday life and of every culture, and thus a real opportunity for building humanity's peace and future."

This language is very different from the discourse at the World Economic Forum. The values of the "Davos culture" largely coincide with those of current Western civilization, which has been principally responsible for spreading these values worldwide. But what grants legitimacy or meaning to these values? If they serve merely as a kind of convention by which the world has by and large agreed to live, they rest on an extremely shaky footing.

This is particularly true when we consider that the values of this international culture generally represent the views of an elite even within the dominant nations. Moreover, an increasing amount of the tension that we are seeing worldwide has to do with widespread *rejection* of these values by cultures influenced by Islam. What Muslims often reject in this Western mind-set is not a different religion but the apparent absence of religious values. Samuel P. Huntington writes, "In Muslim eyes Western secularity, irreligiosity, and hence immorality are worse evils than . . . Western Christianity. . . . In the Cold War the West labeled its opponents 'godless communism'; in the post–Cold War conflict of civilizations Muslims see their opponents as 'the godless West.'"[16]

The solution is not simply to market our values in a more religious fashion. Instead, we should ask whether we can survive as a civilization without a belief in the God who has created the values underlying our civilization. We are all familiar with the lines from the Declaration of Independence: "We hold these truths to be self-evident, that all men are created equal, that they are endowed by their Creator with certain unalienable Rights, that among these are Life, Liberty and the pursuit of Happiness." We frequently forget, however, that these lines explicitly say that "all men are *created* equal" and that "they are endowed *by their Creator*" with these "unalienable Rights." Can our belief in these rights continue to stand without a belief in a God who upholds them or, even more important, whose revelation of love reveals their true meaning?

These issues have long been debated. The philosopher John Locke, whose "Letter Concerning Toleration," written in 1689, is one of the earliest and most celebrated affirmations of religious liberty (and whose ideas were a primary inspiration to our Founding Fathers), asserted that "promises, covenants, and oaths, which are the bonds of human society, can have no hold upon an atheist. The taking away of God, though but even in thought, dissolves all."[17] It would be too extreme, of course, to make these claims about every individual who denies the existence of God, but we can still wonder if a society that does so will be able to hold together.

Speaking to this issue during his visit to Brazil in May 2007, Benedict XVI said, "I do not mean that nonbelievers cannot live a lofty and exemplary morality; I am only saying that a society in which God is absent will not find the necessary consensus on moral values or the strength to live according to the model of these values."[18] Nonetheless, as Jean-François Revel signaled in 1970 with his book *Without Marx or Jesus*, there are elites in both the United States and Europe who are attempting to build cultures where even their Christian "roots" are not acknowledged.

If secular society is no longer rooted in a belief in God, in what is it rooted? Secular society is partly rooted in a belief in *progress*. Many views of progress have been inspired, consciously or unconsciously, by what has been called the "Whig view of history." This term (taken from the name of the predecessor to the British Liberal Party) was coined by the British historian Herbert Butterfield. He applied it (critically) to earlier historians such as Thomas Babington Macaulay, who saw history as the steady march of progress. In 1848, praising the improvements in living standards in England, Macaulay wrote:

The street which now affords to the artisan during the whole night, a secure, a convenient, and a brilliantly lighted walk was, a hundred and sixty years ago, so dark after sunset that he would not have been able to see his hand, so ill paved that he would have run constant risk of breaking his neck, and so ill watched that he would have been in imminent danger of being knocked down and plundered of his small earnings. Every bricklayer who falls from a scaffold, every sweeper of a crossing who is run over by a carriage, may now have his wound dressed and his limbs set with a skill such as, a hundred and sixty years ago, all the wealth of a great lord ... could not have purchased. Some frightful diseases have been extirpated by science; and some have been banished by police.[19]

Macaulay goes on to prophesy:

It may well be, in the twentieth century, that the peasant of Dorsetshire may think himself miserably paid with twenty shillings a week; ... that labouring men may be as little used to dine without meat as they now are to eat rye bread; that sanitary police and medical discoveries may have added several more years to the average length of human life; that numerous comforts and luxuries which are now unknown, or confined to a few, may be within the reach of every diligent and thrifty working man.[20]

Of course, Macaulay's predictions proved correct. Indeed, they have been exceeded. And we can all be grateful for this progress. But we have learned enough since his time to see that his view of history is exceedingly one-sided. For one thing, material progress has its dark side. In his book *Values in a Time of Upheaval*, Joseph Cardinal Ratzinger (now Pope Benedict XVI) writes:

Anyone who looks even at only the last hundred years cannot deny that immense progress has been made in medicine, in technology, and in the understanding and harnessing of the forces of nature, and one may hope for further progress. At the same time, however, the ambivalence of this progress is obvious. Progress is beginning to put Creation—the basis of our existence—at risk; it creates inequality among human beings, and it generates ever new threats to the world and humanity.[21]

Modern advancements have strings attached. For example, while many of the old "frightful diseases" have been wiped out by science, our modern way of living has exposed us to other, perhaps even more frightful, diseases, some of them the result of the "comforts and luxuries" that Macaulay foresaw would someday be available to practically everyone. Thus progress generates "ever new threats" to humanity.

There is another problem with progress viewed materialistically. It denies the value of a transcendent reality in which our daily lives are grounded and which gives them meaning. Consequently, human life is reduced to a meaning and purpose only in reference to *this* world, which is asking of this world something that it does not have the power to give. Ratzinger writes: "If men have nothing more to expect than what this world offers them, and if they may and must demand all this from the state, they destroy both their own selves and every human society."[22] This is true in large measure because history is not the materialistic and impersonal evolution toward something better—history is an event of freedom.

But here, too, freedom is not an absolute value. It cannot be lived in isolation, that is, unhinged from other values such as equality and human dignity. In a tyrannical society, the masters are just as much in bondage as their slaves. As a nation, we have put slavery behind us. But what is slavery other than the ultimate institutionalization of the idea that another human being can be regarded as an object to be used, rather than always regarded as a person to be loved. If there is to be freedom in any meaningful sense, it must be rooted in something higher, and that is morality. Ratzinger observes, "Freedom demands that governments and all those who bear responsibility bow down before a reality that is defenseless and incapable of exercising any coercion: morality."[23]

In defending freedom in this way, Ratzinger invokes a concept that has always been of prime importance in Catholic theology but that has been shunted aside in the current discourse: *natural law*. Praising democratic institutions as they evolved in Britain and the United States, he writes, "In the Anglo-Saxon sphere, democracy was at least partly conceived and realized on the basis of the tradition of natural law and of a fundamental Christian consensus that had a very pragmatic character."[24]

The classic definition of natural law is from St. Thomas Aquinas, who says that it is "nothing else than the rational creature's participation in the divine law."[25] That is, natural law is how human beings understand the eternal laws of the universe as laid down by God. As we experience it, natural law is essentially an inborn and self-evident knowledge of right and wrong.

What are these self-evident truths? The celebrated Christian author C. S. Lewis speaks of an innate sense of right and wrong in his book *The Abolition of Man*. Borrowing a term from the Chinese, he calls this universal law the *Tao*, which means "Nature, the Way, the Road." Lewis explains: "It is the doctrine of objective value, the belief that certain attitudes are really true, and others really false, to the kind of thing the universe is and the kind of things we are."[26] These values are, he stresses, not limited to Christianity; he finds examples of them in sacred literature the world over. These principles include the Golden Rule, duties to parents and elders, duties to children and posterity, justice, mercy, good faith, and veracity. Lewis argues that these values are universal; like the axioms of geometry, they are beyond dispute, and they are self-evident. They are the premises on which all forms of moral reasoning are based, because they are time honored and time tested as the best possible way for people to live in peace and happiness with one another.

Lewis says these values are ultimate, and in a sense he is right. Even so, I believe it is possible to go one step further and say where and in what natural law is grounded, and this truth constitutes what I consider to be the central point of this book. When one of the Pharisees asked, "Teacher, which is the great commandment in the law?" Jesus replied: "You shall love the Lord your God with all your heart, and with all your soul, and with all your mind. This is the great and first commandment. And a second is like it. You shall love your neighbor as yourself. On these two commandments depend all the law and the prophets."[27] Jesus's statement that the "law and the prophets" rest upon these two "commandments" leads to this answer: *the basis of natural law is love.* We might then read St. Thomas Aquinas's definition of natural law a bit differently. If natural law is "nothing else than the rational creature's participation in the divine law," then natural law leads ultimately to nothing else than the rational creature's participation in divine love.

We can see a glimpse of this truth in many places, not all of them in a Christian context. One example is Mitch Albom's remarkable account of the last days of his friend and former college professor Morrie Schwartz in *Tuesdays with Morrie*. Even as he is dying of a rare neurological disease, the old professor cannot stop teaching; only this time he is teaching his greatest lesson. Early in the book there is this exchange:

"Life is a series of pulls back and forth. You want to do one thing, but you are bound to do something else. Something hurts you, yet you know it shouldn't. You take certain things for granted, even when you know you should never take anything for granted.

"A tension of opposites, like a pull on a rubber band. And most of us live somewhere in the middle."

Sounds like a wrestling match, I say.

"A wrestling match." He laughs. "Yes, you could describe life that way."

So which side wins, I ask?

"Which side wins?"

He smiles at me, the crinkled eyes, the crooked teeth.

"Love wins. Love always wins."[28]

A little later, Morrie explains:

"The most important thing in life is to learn how to give out love, and to let it come in."

His voice dropped to a whisper. "Let it come in. We think we don't deserve love, we think if we let it in we'll become too soft. But a wise man named Levine said it right. He said, 'Love is the only rational act.'"[29]

Reading these lines has made a deep impression on me. For twenty-five years, on several occasions each year, I had the opportunity to meet a former professor who, like Morrie, was dying of a debilitating neurological disease during the last years of his life. He, too, continued to teach us life's greatest lessons, even on his last day, as he was dying. But this former professor was not a Jew; he was a Catholic. Of course, I never attended any courses taught by Karol Wojtyla when he was a professor of ethics at the Catholic University of Lublin in Poland. But as a professor at his newly founded Pontifical Institute for Studies on Marriage and Family at the Vatican's Lateran University in Rome, I came to know this man as Pope John Paul II. I participated in faculty meetings with him, private discussions with him, and invitations through the years to participate in Mass with him in his private chapel as well as joining him for breakfasts and lunches. Virtually every one of these occasions was the opportunity for him to elaborate on a central theme of his pontificate. As he wrote in 1981, the year I first met him:

> God created man in His own image and likeness: calling him to existence through love, He called him at the same time for love. God is love and in Himself He lives a mystery of personal loving communion. Creating the human race in His own image and continually keeping it in being, God inscribed in the humanity of man and woman the vocation, and thus the capacity and responsibility, of love and communion. Love is therefore the fundamental and innate vocation of every human being.[30]

John Paul II insisted that a person's life is meaningless without love. Only when this great need, which is at the same time a great calling, is affirmed can the great dignity of each person be clearly seen and respected. It is the vocation to love that not only makes each person, but makes each person human. To say that the vocation to love formed the basis for John Paul II's philosophy of life subtly but profoundly misses the point. The vocation to love quite simply *was* John Paul II's life. What he taught us in so many different ways is that it is also the vocation of each one of us. We know that the vocation to love is written in the heart of each person. What we don't know is why so often it is so difficult to see this reality.

The vocation to love is the only value strong enough to overcome contemporary culture's often consumerist and manipulative view of human relationships. Too often, people are treated as nothing more than objects—of value only because they are seen as being useful to achieve some purpose, whether it is personal, social, or economic. But the person who is the object of our love is of value because he or she is loved, not because he or she is useful or productive. On the contrary, it is often the case that the person is most loved when he or she is *least* useful, for example, in the case of the very young or the very old or the very sick. And we are capable of loving like this because we ourselves have first been loved. This is the lesson of Mother Teresa of Calcutta and many other great saints. It is this vision to which Christianity points. A contemporary Paul, speaking to a modern equivalent of the council of the Areopagus, might well invoke this truth as the basis of all rights and duties. But I believe he would go still further and remind us that love is the very basis of our own being. To be cut off from it is to be cut off from ourselves.

Speaking in 2007, Princeton historian Bernard Lewis said, "There are times in the long history of the human adventure when we have a real turning point, a major change—the end of an era, the beginning of a new era. I am becoming more and more convinced that we are in such an age at the present time— a change in history comparable with such events as the fall of Rome, the discovery of America, and the like."[31] I think John Paul II would have agreed with this assessment. What's more, he would not be discouraged or intimidated by it. Had he been in Lewis's audience that night, I think he would have replied, "Be not afraid," and he would have challenged those there to join him in seeing in this "turning point" the opportunity to build something great: to build a civilization of love on the basis that we are all "God's offspring."

SUGGESTIONS FOR CONTEMPLATION AND ACTION

1. Spend one hour walking around the location of your choice—a city street, a residential neighborhood, even a mall—and make a point of looking at the things you see without mentally attaching price tags to them.

2. Take a person you know reasonably well and ask yourself what he or she is worth. What comes to your mind when you ask this question? If you find yourself thinking solely

in terms of money or property, consider other ways in
which you might estimate the value of this person.

3. Close your eyes and think of the word "civilization."
   What sorts of images or ideas come to your mind? Take
   the inquiry back further. What are the principles on
   which civilization as you conceive it is built?

4. Think back on a time or situation in which you did not
   feel free. Then think of a situation in which you did feel
   free. What are the circumstances that came to your mind?
   Were the limitations imposed on you from outside or by
   you yourself?

5. Sometime in the next week, take one action that will help
   you feel more free. It could involve writing a letter to a
   legislator, speaking your mind in a situation where you
   otherwise might have been silent, or even paying a bill
   that has been weighing on your mind. Note how you feel
   both before and after.

2

A Culture of Suspicion

In 1882, a young parish priest in New Haven, Connecticut, named Michael Joseph McGivney (1852–1890) founded a fraternal society for Catholic men called the Knights of Columbus. Michael Joseph was a first-generation Irish American, the oldest of thirteen children born to Mary and Patrick McGivney, who had both immigrated to America in 1849. We know a good deal about this generation of American Catholics, about the bigotry they faced from the Know-Nothing party, and how they went to work at the toughest jobs in America's industrial and port cities. During the Civil War they filled the ranks of the Union Army and distinguished themselves in units such as the famous "Irish Brigade." And after the war they went back to work in the factories and warehouses and along the wharfs and railways of New England.

In their best-selling biography of Father McGivney, *Parish Priest,* Douglas Brinkley and Julie Fenster describe him in these words: "Calm, mild-mannered, and dutiful, Father McGivney was known in Catholic circles around New England as a pure-hearted reformer. There was, by all accounts, something both stoic and angelic about his nature."[1] At his memorial service in 1890 he was described as "a man of the people" and "zealous of the people's welfare."[2] We generally consider Father McGivney as the young priest who made an extraordinary contribution to the history of Catholicism in North America during the later part of the nineteenth century by founding the Knights of Columbus. Yet, I think that his legacy is not fully appreciated unless he is also seen within the intellectual climate of his time. Father McGivney was, in fact, as a contemporary of some of the greatest intellectual (and most anti-Christian) influences on modern society— philosophers such as Friedrich Nietzsche, Karl Marx, and Sigmund Freud.

I have often reflected on the fact that the Knights of Columbus was founded in the same year that the German philosopher Friedrich Nietzsche (1844–1900) made his now-famous pronouncement "God is dead."[3] He was speaking of what he considered an obvious truth: that for many in Europe it was no longer possible to believe in the Christian God. This idea gradually grew in public awareness until the cover of *Time* magazine on April 8, 1966, featured the stark question in red letters against a black background: "Is God dead?" In Roman Polanski's 1968 horror film *Rosemary's Baby*, Rosemary (played by Mia Farrow), who unbeknownst to her is carrying the child of the Devil, glimpses this issue of *Time* in the waiting room of her obstetrician. Later, when she first sees her baby, Rosemary cries, "Oh God!" One of her Satanist neighbors replies, "God is dead! Long live Satan!" The message is clear: the death of God in human belief opens up an infinite chasm of evil.

Nietzsche did not believe in God in any familiar sense: *"Never, neither indirectly nor directly, neither as a dogma nor as an allegory, has religion yet held any truth."*[4] For him, God was the collective creation of society. At times, he said, societies lose their faith in their gods. Then they find or create new ones, as the late classical world replaced the pagan gods of Olympus with the Christian one.

For Nietzsche, Christianity was far inferior to the Greco-Roman religion that preceded it. At least, he said, the pagan gods gave their believers a sense of inner dignity—an "ideal" to look up to. "Christianity, on the other hand, crushed and shattered man completely." Nietzsche often portrayed Christianity as a religion of slaves. "'Only if you repent will God show you grace'—that would strike a Greek as ridiculous and annoying. He would say: 'Maybe slaves feel that way.'"[5] For Nietzsche, the victory of Christianity was the victory of a slave mentality.

Nietzsche argued for a new way of life based upon the rejection of Christianity, contending that now we must have the courage to live without Christ. For Nietzsche, this courage meant embracing the human condition with naked honesty. "Nothing is true; all is permitted," he wrote.[6] By encountering the universe as it really is, in all its blind indifference, without illusions or manufactured gods, humanity can overcome itself and eventually give rise to what Nietzsche called the "superman."[7]

Nietzsche's influence was far reaching. A generation after Nietzsche's death, the Nazis embraced his concept of the will to power and the superman in their own ideology. Today, we may easily dismiss a philosophy of the "superman." But it would be hard to overestimate the importance of Nietzsche's ideas in twentieth century thought—and in the lives we lead today. For many contemporary secular intellectuals, morals, ideals and reason, are little more than cloaks or masks for naked power: Consequently, they see Christian morality as nothing more than a coercive mechanism limiting human progress, and this mechanism must be dismantled before the dignity and freedom of the individual can be established.

Sigmund Freud (1856–1939), like Nietzsche, regarded religion as inherently preposterous: one of Freud's works is titled *Religion: The Future of an Illusion*. Unlike Nietzsche, however, who cared little about religious experience as such, Freud *did* try to understand religious experience. In another of his works, *Civilization and Its Discontents*, Freud mentions some correspondence with his friend, the French novelist Romain Rolland. Rolland had told him that the true source of religious feeling was "a sensation of 'eternity,' a feeling of something limitless, unbounded, as it were, 'oceanic,'" as Freud describes his friend's views. "One may, [Rolland] thinks, rightly call oneself religious on the ground of this oceanic feeling alone, even if one rejects every belief."[8]

Although Freud could not discover this "oceanic" feeling in his own life, he tried to understand Rolland's perspective. He came to explain it in terms of the early experiences of infancy: "An infant at the breast does not as yet distinguish his ego from the external world as the source of the sensations flowing in upon him. He gradually learns to do so, in response to various promptings." Freud goes on to say that certain people very likely retain some unconscious memories of "limitlessness and of a bond with the universe—the same ideas with which my friend elucidated the 'oceanic' feeling."[9] This would be the source of religious experience.

Freud went on to posit an extremely close connection between God and the father figure. In *Civilization and Its Discontents* he wrote:

> The common man cannot imagine this Providence otherwise than in the figure of an enormously exalted father. Only such a being can understand the needs of the children of men and be softened by their prayers and placated by the signs of their remorse. The whole is so patently infantile, so foreign to reality, that to anyone with a friendly attitude to humanity it is painful to think that the great majority of mortals will never be able to rise above this view of life.[10]

Here, too, we find an element of suspicion. Freud's view, put as simply as possible, was that human beings are fundamentally composed of some elementary, instinctual drives. But as people experience the world, they soon come up against the unpleasant fact that they cannot express all their desires. They must repress them, and one of the most common ways of doing so is by imagining a kind of father figure—a God—who prohibits these behaviors. This repression leads to the state of mental anxiety and dysfunction that Freud called *neurosis*.

Freud's impact on modern thought has been monumental. Although many of his ideas have been modified or rejected by his successors, his work is still regarded as the starting point for modern psychology. His ideas, filtered down through innumerable books and articles that quote him, have made their way into ordinary language. When we speak of "ego" or "libido," or when we call someone a "neurotic," we are using Freud's terms.

It would be possible to invoke many other modern thinkers whose criticisms of Christianity echo those of Nietzsche and Freud. In a famous passage, Karl Marx (1818–1883) wrote:

Man is no abstract being squatting outside the world. Man is *the world of man*—state, society. This state and this society produce religion, which is an inverted consciousness of the world, because they are an inverted world. . . .

Religious suffering is, at one and the same time, the expression of real suffering and a protest against real suffering. Religion is the sigh of the oppressed creature, the heart of a heartless world, and the soul of soulless conditions. It is the opium of the people.

The abolition of religion as the illusory happiness of the people is the demand for their real happiness. To call on them to give up their illusions about their condition is to call on them to give up a condition that requires illusions. The criticism of religion is, therefore, in embryo, the criticism of that vale of tears of which religion is the halo.[11]

For all their differences, there are some striking resemblances among these thinkers. In the first place, they regard religion— especially Christianity—as fundamentally illusory. They do not debate about the existence of God. The idea that there could be a God is dismissed out of hand. For them, the real issue is to accurately understand the human person. They regard religion as nothing more than a social mechanism, a means of managing the discontents of individuals as they are forced to live together. For Freud, this process is to some degree benign, or at any rate inevitable; it is what enables society to function. Marx and Nietzsche see a more sinister motive. For Nietzsche, Christianity arose out of the "resentment" of the strong by the weak. For Marx, religion is the drug that the slaves of industrial civilization take to dull the pain of their bondage.

In a series of lectures delivered at Yale University in 1961, the French philosopher Paul Ricoeur described Marx, Nietzsche, and Freud as "three masters of suspicion." He called them "three great destroyers" whose methods have had a widespread impact on reducing the influence of Christianity in society.

For these "masters of suspicion," their own alternative interpretations of human behavior are held to be more consistent with human dignity and human freedom than that presented by Christianity.[12] The traditional Christian view—that human beings are endowed with immortal souls and are able through reason to understand certain eternal truths about God and the universe—is dismissed as childish fantasy. When God is doubted, every tenet of Christianity either must be able to be explained with natural reasons or must be discounted as false—every tenet, including love.

For Freud, the Christian way of life and especially what John Paul II would later describe as the vocation to love is irrational. It distorts human nature and frustrates fundamental human desires. Here is Freud commenting on the commandment "Thou shall love thy neighbor as thyself":

> Let us adopt a naïve attitude towards it, as though we were hearing it for the first time; we shall be unable then to suppress a feeling of surprise and bewilderment. Why should we do it? What good will it do us? But, above all, how shall we achieve it? How can it be possible? My love is something valuable to me which I ought not to throw away without reflection.[13]

Ricoeur explained Freud's difficulty with Christianity in this way:

> Why does man fail to be happy? Why is man as a cultural being dissatisfied? [Freud's] analysis here reaches its turning point. Confronting man is an absurd commandment: to love one's neighbor as oneself; an impossible demand: to love one's enemies; a dangerous order: to turn the other cheek. These precepts squander love, put a premium on being bad, and lead to ruin anyone imprudent enough to obey them.[14]

Nietzsche, Freud, and Marx each offered alternatives to Christianity's view of the world by focusing not on the existence of God but on ways to promote human progress. For Nietzsche, this centered on the "will to power" for the sake of the coming superman. Marx advocated a political economics that would lead to a future utopia. Freud proposed a new understanding of human psychology and sexuality. Each argued from a different perspective, but always to the same conclusion: Christianity is not adequate for understanding human nature, freedom, or dignity. Christianity, they said, is not the truth that sets people free. It is what keeps him enslaved.

What Ricoeur perceived as a philosophical trend in the early 1960s has emerged today with all the force of a paradigmatic change in culture. It would not be an exaggeration to say that the "masters of suspicion" have largely succeeded today (in some places much more dramatically than in others) in creating a new "culture of suspicion" in which Christianity and its values are increasingly marginalized by contemporary Western society. This culture is much more pronounced in many nations in Europe than it is in the United States. But even in the United States its influence is increasingly apparent. Although this new culture may not embrace Marx's language, which describes religion as the "opium of the people," it simply treats religion like a dangerous and destructive drug.

The present era is not the first one in which Christianity has had to confront philosophical challenges. Paul preaching at the Areopagus is perhaps the earliest example and involved, at least in part, the same issue: an adequate understanding of the nature and dignity of each person. Of course, Paul's critique of classical pagan culture was developed throughout the early centuries of the church (most prominently by St. Augustine), and it rested precisely on the claim that it is Christ and Christ alone who fully reveals man to himself. Therefore, as worthy as the pagan philosophers were, their view of the human person was ultimately insufficient to adequately understand the nature, dignity, and destiny of each man and woman.

The Enlightenment of the eighteenth century marks a reversal of this dynamic, which, we might say, reaches its high point with the masters of suspicion. Now it is Christianity that is under attack with a critique charging that it in turn misconstrues human nature. This inadequate understanding leads to the imposition of an artificial and false morality that restrains humanity's freedom and arrests its development.

John Paul II and Benedict XVI have responded to this challenge by taking St. Augustine's tack, saying in effect, "We have studied the new 'pagan' philosophers and have found *their* view of the human person to be inadequate." Both popes have taken their cue from the teachings of Vatican II, particularly the insight of the pastoral constitution *Gaudium et Spes*: "The truth is that only in the mystery of the incarnate Word does the mystery of man take on light."[15] Indeed, virtually every encyclical written by John Paul II makes some reference to this statement of the Second Vatican Council.

On reading this sentence, one's first impression may be that it is simply stating the obvious: of course, a Christian would be expected to say something like that. But this statement is not understood by John Paul II as a mere matter of abstract theology; it touches each of us to the very center of our lives. We cannot understand ourselves without acknowledging the presence of Christ at the center of our own being. It radically changes our perspective on human nature to think of ourselves as creatures centered in Christ and reflecting his image. At the very least, it takes the other aspects of human nature that we have glimpsed here—the libido, the will to power, the economic impulse—and subordinates them to a higher power that is both within us and beyond us.

One might consider the entire mission of the pontificate of John Paul II as an effort to teach this truth, beginning with his first encyclical, *Redemptor Hominis* ("Redeemer of Humanity"): "Christ the Redeemer fully reveals man to himself."[16] That is to say, human self-knowledge in the fullest sense is not possible without Christ. What may be most remarkable about John Paul's vision is the great emphasis it places on the profound dignity and exaltation of every person. He draws our attention to a passage from *Gaudium et Spes*: "Human nature, by the very fact that it was assumed, not absorbed, in [Christ], has been raised in us also to a dignity beyond compare. For, by his Incarnation, he, the son of God, *in a certain way united himself with each man*."[17] (Emphasis Pope John Paul II's own in his encyclical) This "unity" calls each Christian to recognize in a more profound way the dramatic equality of every human being.

Among the most powerful passages of *Redemptor Hominis* are those in which the pope speaks to the condition of the modern world, including the issue of freedom. Freedom was certainly the aim of the thinkers we have explored in this chapter, each of whom thought he was helping to free individuals from bonds imposed by society. For John Paul II, freedom does not lie in this direction.

Man's true freedom is not found in everything that the various ous systems and individuals see and propagate as freedom. . . .

All too often freedom is confused with the instinct for individual or collective interest or with the instinct for combat and domination, whatever be the ideological colours with which they are covered. Obviously these instincts exist and are operative, but no truly human economy will be possible unless they are taken up, directed and dominated by the deepest powers in man, which decide the true culture of peoples.[18]

The phrase "the deepest powers in man" is particularly striking. If we were to turn to each of the masters of suspicion and ask them to locate the deepest powers of man, they would point to the instinctual level: the libido, the will to power, the drive for economic liberation. John Paul II, echoing the entirety of the Christian tradition, challenges this view. He admits that these instincts are "still operative," but he also says there are yet deeper powers in man that are (or should be) in charge: "We see Christ as the one who brings man freedom based on truth, frees man from what curtails, diminishes and as it were breaks off this freedom at its root, in man's soul, his heart and his conscience."[19]

It is only this connection with these "deepest powers" that guarantees true freedom. Otherwise we are left merely with "the instinct for individual or collective interest or with the instinct for combat and domination." If the history of the human race has taught us nothing else, it should at least have taught us that freedom in this instinctual sense is utterly illusory. It is the freedom of the tyrant, who is caged by the fear and hatred of his own subjects; of the libertine, who is the slave of his desires; of the nihilist, who cries with Nietzsche, "Nothing is true; all is permitted."

True freedom, as John Paul II stresses, is grounded in the true and the good, and these in turn are grounded in Wisdom and Love. For Christians, it is Christ through whom "the world ... recovers again its original link with the divine source of Wisdom and Love. Man cannot live without love. He remains a being that is incomprehensible for himself, his life is senseless, if love is not revealed to him, if he does not encounter love, if he does not experience it and make it his own, if he does not participate intimately in it. This, as has already been said, is why Christ the Redeemer 'fully reveals man to himself'."[20]

Not only is this the authentic root of freedom, it is the very root of human nature itself. Because Christ has united himself to each person, he has opened the possibility of the greatest freedom—the freedom to realize the deepest desire of the human heart: the desire to love in a way that is true and in a way that may find a love that is true in return. This is only possible because we have first been loved by the one whose love is truth itself.

John Paul II stresses that he does not mean to limit this vision to a narrow sectarian perspective. In the same encyclical he writes, "The life of Christ speaks, also, to many who are not capable of repeating with Peter: 'You are the Christ, the Son of the living God' (Matt. 16:16). He, the Son of the living God, speaks to people also as Man: it is his life that speaks, his humanity, his fidelity to the truth, his all-embracing love."[21] John Paul II emphasizes the universal embrace of Christ's love. He notes, "With each man without any exception whatever . . . Christ is in a way united, even when man is unaware of it."[22]

It is often said that a pope's first encyclical is an occasion for the new pontiff to state the major theme (or themes) of his pontificate. It is extraordinary that Benedict XVI would begin his first encyclical, *Deus Caritas Est* (*God Is Love*) with these words from the *First Letter of John:* "God is love, and he who abides in love abides in God, and God abides in him."[23] His encyclical, issued on Christmas Day, 2005, is a treatise on the nature of love. If each of us is called to a vocation of love, what does this entail? What does this require of us? *Deus Caritas Est* offers answers to these questions. But the encyclical begins by addressing an even more fundamental issue: does Christianity accurately understand the nature of human love and therefore also adequately understand the nature of the human person?

Practically all the philosophers and theologians who have dealt with the nature of love have emphasized one central fact: there are many kinds of love. "So we need to ask," the pope writes, "are all these forms of love basically one, so that love, in its many and varied manifestations, is ultimately a single reality, or are we merely using the same word to designate totally different realities?"[24]

Benedict replies that there are essentially two forms of love: *eros* and *agape:* passionate, sexual love and the dispassionate, unconditional love of Christianity.[25] Then, in an extraordinary reference (and as if in some way to specifically address the "masters of suspicion"), the pope directly responds to one of Nietzsche's fundamental criticisms of Christianity:

> In the critique of Christianity which began with the Enlightenment and grew progressively more radical, this new element [i.e., the Christian teaching of *agape*] was seen as something thoroughly negative. According to Friedrich Nietzsche, Christianity had poisoned *eros*, which for its part, while not completely succumbing, gradually degenerated into vice. Here the German philosopher was expressing a widely held perception: doesn't the Church, with all her commandments and prohibitions, turn to bitterness the most precious thing in life?[26]

Benedict XVI replies by saying that the Catholic Church has never denounced *eros* as such, but merely its debased and dehumanized forms—allowing oneself to be subjugated by mere instinct or regarding the other not as a person but as an object. "Eros needs to be disciplined and purified if it is to provide not just fleeting pleasure, but a certain foretaste of the pinnacle of our existence, of that beatitude for which our whole being yearns."[27]

The discipline of which the encyclical speaks is not repression or denial but the purification of sexual love. This involves "a real discovery of the other, moving beyond the selfish character that prevailed earlier. Love now becomes concern and care for the other. No longer is it self-seeking, a sinking in the intoxication of happiness; instead it seeks the good of the beloved: it becomes renunciation and it is ready, and even willing, for sacrifice."[28] This maturing *eros* then seeks to become "definitive ... both in the sense of exclusivity (this particular person alone) and in the sense of being 'for ever.'"[29]

Benedict XVI also stresses that we must trace love back to its fundamental source.

> Anyone who wishes to give love must also receive love as a gift. Certainly, as the Lord tells us, one can become a source from which rivers of living water flow (cf. Jn 7:37–38). Yet to become such a source, one must constantly drink anew from the original source, which is Jesus Christ, from whose pierced heart flows the love of God (cf. Jn 19:34).[30]

Thus, like his predecessor, Benedict XVI stresses that at the heart of love lies Christ himself. The answer of both popes is that Jesus, in revealing the way in which God is love, shows each person the way of love and therefore the way of freedom and personal fulfillment.

Some intellectuals may say that this focus on these masters of suspicion is antiquated. All of them were born in the nineteenth century, and the youngest, Freud, died in 1939. Hasn't modern— or rather postmodern—thought progressed since then? A full answer to this objection would be extremely intricate and technical, but the short answer is that the currently fashionable school of postmodernism is heavily indebted to the masters of suspicion and has even taken their method of suspicion to its "logical" conclusion. In any event, it is interesting that Benedict XVI would think enough of the continuing relevance of Nietzsche and his criticism of Christianity to directly respond to it in his first encyclical.

The Christian vision set out by the popes offers a very different picture. They do not deny the presence and the power of instinctual drives, but they also insist that these drives do not constitute our deepest nature. If we go past these drives—admittedly, not always an easy task—we reach the true center of our being, where we find Christ, who bestows upon us his wisdom and love. Having reached this point, we can reach out to the world not with the urge for domination and mastery, but with kindness and gentleness.

How can we know which of these visions is true? The intricacies of suspicion sound brilliant and compelling, but can they take us to the best and highest in ourselves?

Paul Ricoeur accurately described our challenge in his description of Freud's view of Christianity. "Confronting man is an absurd commandment: to love one's neighbor as oneself; an impossible demand: to love one's enemies; a dangerous order: to turn the other cheek."[31] An absurd commandment? A dangerous order? An impossible demand?

It is here that the civilization of love directly confronts the new culture of suspicion.

Is it possible to live a life dedicated to a vocation to love that opens up true freedom and leads to personal fulfillment? Can Christians demonstrate by their personal example, as well as by that of their families and communities, that such a way of life is possible? The answers to these questions ultimately will not be found in the pages of any book, but in the daily lives of those who live a vocation to love. The proof of the Christian worldview is to be found in the living witness of Christians.

Suggestions for Contemplation and Action

1. What role does doubt play in your life? Where do you find yourself most (and least) likely to doubt or trust? Look back on your life and see what role doubt has played in it. Ask yourself honestly whether, on the whole, you should have been more doubtful or more trusting in the past. What would the consequences have been?

2. Spend a day looking at your own use of power. Examine how much power—in a literal, physical sense—it takes you to accomplish the tasks of the day. Be aware of the amount of energy it takes to do even very simple things like walking into another room or starting a car. (It would be most helpful to do this exercise while carrying on your life exactly as you ordinarily would.)

3. Once you have done this, spend another day looking at other ways of using power. What power or influence do you have over others? What power do they have over you? Are you more likely to dominate or be dominated? When you do use power, do you use it wisely? With this exercise, as with all the practices suggested in this book, it is extremely important to be totally and ruthlessly honest with yourself.

4. Think back to at least three times in your life when you genuinely felt loved. What were the occasions? What did it feel like? Does your memory of these experiences tell you something about what love is?

5. Think back to three other times in your life when you genuinely showed love for someone else. What were the occasions? What did it feel like? How does this compare to the times when you felt loved?

3

Craftsmen of a New Humanity

On January 17, 2004, a concert unique in the history of music was performed at the Vatican. Called the Papal Concert of Reconciliation, it was an event created to inspire unity among the great Abrahamic faiths—Christianity, Judaism, and Islam—and the audience included not only Pope John Paul II but the chief rabbi and the imam of Rome. The concert brought together musicians from Germany, England, Poland, Turkey, and the United States to perform before an audience gathered from every continent as well as almost every nation and religious faith on the planet. The Pittsburgh Symphony Orchestra, under the direction of Gilbert Levine, performed movements of Gustav Mahler's magnificent *Second Symphony in C Minor*. For this symphony, Mahler had taken for his inspiration *Dziady*, the dramatic poem by Poland's great poet and playwright Adam Mickiewicz, to create one of the nineteenth century's most profound works of spiritual artistry.

The Knights of Columbus had provided the financial support to make the concert a reality, and because of that, I had gotten to know Gilbert Levine and discussed with him on repeated occasions the vision inspiring the concert as well as many of its details. There was even the opportunity to meet with John Paul II and express in a personal way our support for this important initiative.

That evening, after listening to the choir and soloists sing, "With wings that I wrested for myself, in the fervent struggle of love, I shall fly away to the light which no eye pierced," everyone waited to hear what the pope would say at the conclusion of the performance. As it turned out, he spoke not only of the role of music in fostering mutual understanding among people of different cultures and religions but of the need for courage in the search for peace. He ended with words directed to the heart of each one there: *Omnia vincit amor*: "Love conquers all."

Some may have dismissed those three words as the poetic response of one Polish poet to the words set to music of an earlier poet of Poland. But that evening, the pope was not simply turning a phrase; he was being as practical as he knew how to be. For him, those three words were not poetry but realpolitik.

That evening, the pope may well have been thinking of the historical context of Mahler's great work. Mahler was of Jewish extraction, and Mickiewicz, the source of inspiration for this symphony, is the great national poet of Poland, as Shakespeare is for England and Dante for Italy. Calling for Polish national liberation in 1848, Mickiewicz had written: "In the nation everyone is a citizen. All citizens are equal before the law and before the administration. To the Jew, our elder brother, [we must show] esteem and help on his path towards eternal welfare and in all matters, equal rights."[1] John Paul II must also have remembered how in his own youth in Wadowice, Poland, in 1938, his teacher Mr. Gebhardt read these words to his class the day after anti-Semitic rioting had broken out, telling the class, "I hope none of my students are to be numbered among last night's hooligans. I am speaking to you not as a history teacher but as a Pole. What happened has nothing to do with the tradition of our Fatherland."[2] In a very literal sense, love *is* realpolitik.

It is the unique contribution of Christianity to have elevated love to the center of human life. Love, of course, has always been known to human beings, and humans have always expressed love to friends and family. As we have seen with the two greatest commandments, it was implicit in the Hebrew revelation, but it was not entirely explicit. And while love was praised by the Greek and Roman philosophers, for them it often seemed to be merely one value among many other values. It was Jesus Christ who revealed to humanity that it is love that lies at the center of the universe, that, in Dante's words, it is love that "moves the sun and the other stars."[3]

But why? Why should love, out of all the values and qualities in the universe, enjoy this privileged position as the source and mover of all things? All religions begin by asserting the existence of a power greater than ourselves, greater than all the forces of nature, visible and invisible, and which has given birth to these forces. For many religions, this power is ultimately impersonal. It is an energy, a dynamic—what the *Star Wars* films call "the Force." The Chinese speak of it as the *Tao*. For Buddhists, it is the primordial nature of mind. For Western philosophers such as Martin Heidegger, it is "Being." But Christianity differs from these views in one fundamental sense: it teaches that this Higher Power is ultimately *personal*. God is not an impersonal force like magnetism or electricity. God is in some ineffable way like us as persons and relates to us as persons. Genesis tells us that man and woman were made in the "image" and "likeness" of God.[4] It is this "image" and "likeness" that, in a sense, provides a frame of reference that makes possible some understanding of the divine mystery and permits a "personal" relationship with God. In Christianity, God is revealed to exist in a mysterious unity of Three Persons, whose mutual relationship is love.

Divine love, then, implies an *other*. This revelation of a God who exists in a personal communion of love reveals to us profound mystery. Love involves (at least) two persons, two selves. To be two, they must in some way be separate. Yet they cannot be totally separate; otherwise they would have nothing to do with each other; they would not even be aware of each other's existence.

There must be a unity, and yet at the same time there must be difference—both symmetry and asymmetry. Because of the analogous nature between God's love and human love, human love retains the requirements of symmetry and asymmetry. So love in some mysterious fashion both separates and connects two individual selves. It *separates* the two because it does not seek to engulf them or destroy them as separate entities. It *connects* them because, by their very nature, they are directed toward another person in a way that enables them to have a loving relationship with each other. And this relationship is fundamentally good. It is satisfying and pleasing and joyful for both.

Thus we might say that the "structure" of human existence is love, given to us in the very form of creation by the God who is love. The world as we know it would not be possible without love. Without this structure of love, everything either would have collapsed long ago into an indeterminate mass or would have been incarcerated in a prison of isolation. It is love and its structure that makes it possible for our world to exist at all. And the first human sign of this structure of love is that man was created in a unity with difference—man and woman.

To some degree, any examination of the human experience becomes a search for origins and causes. In the seventeenth century, the French philosopher René Descartes sought to establish a firm grounding for knowledge. He was challenged by the idea that there was no certainty in the world—all knowledge was relative and subject to doubt. Descartes understood that such relativism would also affect society's values, cutting society adrift from universal principles. He hoped to recover one clear principle of certain knowledge in an attempt to rebuild confidence in reason. He thought that if he could find one universally true principle—not subject to doubt—he could build upon that principle with other equally true principles to more fully grasp reality. After much consideration, Descartes proposed to begin with a simple assertion as a key to understanding humanity's condition: "I think, therefore I am." And with this simple sentence, Descartes changed the history of philosophy and human knowledge.

Today, in a similar way, we confront a problem like the one that challenged Descartes. We are challenged by the assertion of moral relativism—that there are no longer any universal moral principles that can guide a world with so many diverse cultures, religions, and philosophies. And we have moved beyond Descartes' simple trust in the power of intellect. Yet, John Paul II has proposed a principle that is both universal and certain in the hope of overcoming this global challenge, a principle that, if we rely on Descartes' formula, provides us with an even more profound insight: "I love, therefore I am." Or perhaps even more profoundly: "I have first been loved, therefore I am."

As we unfortunately know, however, love does not characterize all human relationships. Its opposite is hatred. In Christian terms, we may also think of love's opposite as *sin*. Although God has granted us the free will to accept or reject his love, it is part of the nature of the universe that rejection of love will lead to pain. We are free to reject love, but we don't have the power to reject it and still be happy. We see this truth in ordinary life, when individuals, for whatever reasons, refuse human companionship and grow more hostile and embittered.

The same is true in spiritual life. Christianity stresses that it is we who reject God, not God who rejects us. Many have been puzzled by Christ's statement about the "blasphemy against the [Holy] Spirit" that "will not be forgiven."[5] John Paul II points out that this "blasphemy" consists precisely in rejecting God's love.

Man cannot get back onto his feet unaided: he needs the help of the Holy Spirit. If he refuses this help, he commits what Christ called "the blasphemy against the Spirit," the sin which "will not be forgiven" (Mt 12:31). Why will it not be forgiven? Because it means there is no desire for pardon. Man refuses the love and mercy of God, since he believes himself to be God. He believes himself to be capable of self-sufficiency.[6]

The Russian philosopher Vladimir Solovyov (1853–1900) offers a fascinating perspective on human self-sufficiency in his treatise *The Meaning of Love*. He points out that we tend to regard ourselves as creatures having absolute value—a value that cannot be reduced to other goals or ends. And we are right to do so. "In every human being there is something absolutely irreplaceable," he writes, "and one cannot value oneself too highly.[7]

This statement may seem peculiar, even arrogant, but of course Solovyov is right. Each of us, as a child of God, *does* have absolute significance and worth. The problem, as Solovyov goes on to say, is not that we overvalue ourselves but that we undervalue everyone else.[8] For Solovyov, love is the answer to this problem. Love does not ask us to despise ourselves, but rather to go past the narrow boundaries of the self and to recognize, not only intellectually but in our hearts, the absolute value and worth of every person.

These reflections lead us to see that there cannot be true love without an equal respect for freedom. If another individual has absolute worth, it follows that he or she must have the freedom to realize and manifest that worth. Love carries with it the responsibility to respect the freedom and dignity of each individual. As the Swiss theologian Hans Urs von Balthasar wrote, "Only a philosophy of freedom and love can account for our existence." The dignity of human existence can only be adequately understood "in terms of love—and not in terms of consciousness, or spirit, or knowledge, or power, or desire, or usefulness."[9] Each of us, then, has a vocation to love.

A vocation is a calling, a kind of profession or occupation. Today we live in a world where professions and occupations are becoming more and more specialized. Knowledge has multiplied so much that any one person can only master a small sliver of it, even in a single discipline. This enables us to accomplish techno-logical wonders that previous eras could only dream of, but it runs the risk of confining each person to a narrow piece of turf. Someone who is restricted to a very limited task may find it hard to see his or her relation to the whole. For many, this has led to a sense of discouragement and disaffection.

It can be hard to see the meaning and purpose of life when one feels like a single blade of grass in a field that stretches farther than the eye can see. But if we can change our perspective and see our ultimate vocation as one of love and of manifesting that love in whatever circumstances we happen to find ourselves, the pic-ture becomes far brighter. We regain the possibility of realizing our own absolute worth—as well as the worth of others—because we recognize that it is neither we ourselves nor society that has established that worth. Rather it is God who has done so, and he has done so through love. We may call this perspective "Christian personalism."

At the center of Christian personalism is a moral view of human dignity that is inalienable because it has been established by God. While this perspective has many roots, its greatest con-temporary foundation in Catholic thought is the Second Vatican Council, especially *Gaudium et Spes*, with its statement that it is "only in the mystery of the Word made flesh that the mystery of man truly becomes clear."[10] This proclamation anchors the dig-nity and freedom of the human person squarely within the event of the Incarnation: God has placed his final seal upon our dignity and worth by becoming one of us.

Throughout his tenure as pope, John Paul II developed the Christian personalism of the Second Vatican Council through numerous encyclicals, which are letters addressed by the pope to all the bishops of the church, beginning with his first, *Redemptor Hominis*. These encyclicals constitute a substantial body of magis-terial teaching on the nature and dignity of the person that is in-dispensable to fostering Catholic identity. The pope wrote, for example, "The Redemption that took place through the Cross has definitively restored his dignity to man and given back meaning to his life in the world, a meaning that was lost to a considerable extent because of sin."[11] His encyclicals also provide a view of the person as rational, moral, and free. They call the individual to "an honest relationship with regard to truth as a condition for authentic freedom" and warn us to avoid "every kind of illusory freedom, every superficial unilateral freedom, every freedom that fails to enter into the whole truth about man and the world."[12] This understanding is the foundation of Catholic teaching on matters of family life, social justice, and peace.

It is certainly possible to affirm these values for oneself and live by them regardless of what anyone else may think. But this, too, can lead to a sense of isolation, and in any case it is not the whole story. In his *Notes towards the Definition of Culture*, T. S. Eliot reminds us that we can consider culture in three different but related senses—the individual, the group, and the whole society. Eliot emphasizes the importance of understanding that there are certain aims appropriate to the individual, others to the group, and still others to the society at large.

The Christian is challenged to influence culture on each of these levels. Each person is called to be in a real sense a "culture of one" in regard to personal values. Each Christian is also called to make a significant contribution to the community of Christians of which he is one part. In this way each can help to build the culture of the Christian community through work in the parish or church-related associations. Eliot maintains that the relationship between religion and culture is so strong and that every culture's development is so interconnected to religion that he even says that "the culture of a people [is] an incarnation of its religion."[13] If this is even partially true, it has important consequences for every religious believer and especially Christians. A Christian who takes seriously the development of his own personal "culture of one" and also assists in the building up of the spiritual community to which he belongs makes a significant contribution to the cultural development of his society at large. Eliot, of course, was one of the great poets and intellectuals of the twentieth century and was awarded the Nobel Prize for Literature in 1948. But in this he was being extraordinarily practical. By looking at influences on culture in this way, Eliot was emphasizing the new democratic nature of culture in our time: culture is not only influenced by cultural elites such as poets, journalists, professors, or artists. Culture is also influenced by what millions of people do every day in their own lives and those of their families and neighbors.

Interestingly, Eliot concluded his discussion on culture with an examination of education, which he found had among its purposes both the "formation of character" of the student and the transmission of culture. Indeed, it is precisely through the transmission of culture that the student's character is largely formed. If the nexus between the individual, the religious community, and society as a whole is broken, the entire culture runs the risk of withering and dying.

The French author and former minister of culture François Mauriac once wrote of an extraordinary episode he experienced during the German occupation of France in World War II. Mauriac stated that of all the things he had witnessed during the occupation, no image remained as vividly impressed upon him as the sight of hundreds of Jewish schoolchildren being separated from their mothers by Nazi soldiers and shipped away by train to unknown destinations. Later they learned the children had been sent to Nazi death camps. Mauriac recalled:

> I believe that on that day, I first became aware of the mystery of iniquity whose revelation was to mark the end of one era and the beginning of another. The dream conceived by Western man in the eighteenth century, whose dawn he thought he had glimpsed in 1789 [with the French

Revolution], and which until August 2, 1914 [the beginning of World War I], had become stronger with the
advent of the Enlightenment and the discoveries of science—that dream vanished finally for me before those
trainloads of small children.[14]

For Mauriac, the European experience of the two world wars
and the horrors of Nazi occupation and the Holocaust marked a
profound shift in the way he viewed European culture. What followed for Mauriac and for millions of other Europeans was a collapse of confidence in the assumptions of European society since
the Enlightenment regarding the inevitability of progress, the
perfectibility of humanity, and, perhaps most important, the ultimate triumph of reason and democracy. This modern secular idea
of the inevitable progress of the good society, what historian Carl
Becker described so well as *The Heavenly City of the Eighteenth-Century
Philosophers,*[15] symbolically ended in anguish at Auschwitz and the
other death camps. In its place followed a new sense of isolation
and futility portrayed in the postwar novels of Albert Camus such
as *The Stranger* and *The Plague* as well as in Elie Wiesel's gripping
account of his time as a youth in the Auschwitz death camp,
Night.

But such spiritual emptiness was apparent between the two
world wars, and it was not confined to the European continent.
Thomas Merton reflects about his time at the University of Cambridge during the 1930s: "What was wrong with this place, with
all these people? Why was everything so empty? . . . It seemed to
me that Cambridge, and, to some extent, the whole of England,
were pretending, with an elaborate and intent and conscious, and
perhaps in some cases a courageous effort, to act as if it were alive.
And it took a lot of acting."

Merton characterizes the spiritual emptiness of Cambridge by
telling of a friend of his named Mike, "a beefy and red-faced and

noisy youth who came from somewhere in Wales. . . , full of loud laughter and well-meaning exclamations." A great eater and drinker and girl chaser, Mike was fond of putting his fist through windows. But his hearty exterior must have concealed some deeper discomfort. "The next year I heard how he ended up. The porter, or somebody, went down into the showers, under the buildings of the Old Court at Clare [College], and found Mike hanging by his neck from a rope slung over one of the pipes, with his big hearty face black with the agony of strangulation. He had hanged himself."[16]

Merton, who spent much of his youth in England, stresses that he does not necessarily mean to apply his statements to the British nation as a whole, but certainly this malaise seems to characterize much of its intellectual elite.

Contrast this picture with some observations by Stephen Ambrose in his book *To America: Personal Reflections of an Historian*:

> In my interviews with World War II veterans, they would sometimes tell me that the reason they fought was they had learned as children the difference between right and wrong and they didn't want to live in a world in which wrong prevailed, so they fought. . . . At the core, the American citizen soldier—unlike those from Germany or the Soviet Union or Japan or elsewhere—knew the difference between right and wrong.[17]

That the "greatest generation" went to war with confidence that right would triumph was no accident of history. Perhaps the most important factor in building this confidence was the moral character of their education. Many in the "greatest generation" were educated in Catholic schools. In those days, however, even the secular public-school system still reflected the influence of a deep-seated sense of Christian morals. The "greatest generation" may have also been one of the greatest examples of what an educational system that built character by transmitting its moral culture can produce.

In American education at that time, this influence was exemplified by William McGuffey's *Eclectic Readers,* first published in 1836. They are among the most popular texts ever used in the United States and have sold more than 120 million copies in four editions. Written by a professor of languages at Ohio's Miami University (he ended his career as professor of moral philosophy at the University of Virginia), the *Readers* were composed of lessons such as "Dare to Do Right," "Omnipotence of God," and "The Righteous Never Forsaken."[18]

One typical lesson contains a narrative written in the person of a professor who sails home after a five-year absence. During his voyage, he is swept off the deck, and as he flails about in the water, he says, "I felt that Almighty God had done this.... I gnashed my teeth and cursed myself—and, with bitter names and tears, blasphemed the name of God." He watches his ship sail off in the distance and gives himself up for lost. "I now felt myself indeed dying. A calm came over me. I prayed devoutly for forgiveness of my sins, and for all my friends on earth." He feels he is "sinking down and down an unfathomable depth, which I thought was Death." Then he hears a voice saying, "Praise the Lord," and finds himself on the deck of another ship that has rescued him. "I had been picked up, apparently dead and cold. The hand of God was there."[19]

The contemporary reader who encounters this lesson is struck by several things. The story is melodramatic, certainly, and its language dated, yet for all that, it retains a strange narrative power. Then there is the remarkable sophistication of its vocabulary and style compared with our current standards (this particular story was written for the upper grades of grammar school). Most remarkable, perhaps, it unabashedly draws a clear moral, even theological, lesson. The professor, swept off the deck by accident, first blames and curses God, then reaches a stage of resignation and repentance, and finally is rescued. There is drama not only in the story's action but in the moral struggle of the protagonist.

Unfortunately, in the years since the mid-twentieth century, the value of public education has been eroded by secularism, relativism, and moral uncertainty. A lesson like this one would not be read in public schools today. It would arouse too many controversies. But the need to form a solid moral core in children and youth is no less important today. There can only be one way to build the relationships necessary for community and culture. We must provide an educational environment in which the spiritual, moral, and intellectual capacities of every person can be realized.

This is not a call for a return to simple moralism. Our world is far too complex. But as psychologist Robert Coles reminds us, the moral life and moral intelligence of children still can and *should* be developed in the classroom,[20] and Catholic schools are uniquely qualified to provide this kind of moral leadership precisely because Catholic schools have a unique tradition of respecting the dignity of every student. In a remarkable study of Catholic education published by Harvard University Press, titled *Catholic Schools and the Common Good*, the authors maintain that Christian *personalism* is one of the most important aspects of Catholic schools that make them very different from public schools:

Christian personalism calls for humaneness in the myriad of mundane social interactions that make up daily life. Crucial to advancing personalism is an extended role for teachers that encourages staff to care about both the kind of people students become as well as the facts, skills, and knowledge they acquire. Moreover, personalism is a communal norm for the school—the kind of behavior modeled by teachers and held out as an ideal for students. As such, personalism is valued not only because it is an effective device to engage students in academic work but also because it signifies a moral conception of social behavior in a just community. As such, personalism makes claims on human endeavors to act, beyond individual interest, toward a greater good.[21]

Consequently, in the future we can hope that Catholic education will take on increasing importance. The next generation of Catholics may well be distinguished by their being the ones who "know the difference between right and wrong" and, when put to the test, will "dare to do right."

Shortly after the Concert for Reconciliation, I had occasion to pick up and read again John Paul II's Message for the 2001 World Day of Peace. It is titled *Dialogue Between Cultures for a Civilization of Love and Peace*.[22] Ironically, it must have been written during the same time that preparations were well under way for the terrorist attack of September 11. Yet, because of those attacks and what has followed, the pope's words take on an even greater importance. John Paul II concluded his message with a consideration of the value of education and what he described as "an appeal to young people."

In regard to education, the pope wrote,

In order to build the civilization of love, dialogue between cultures must . . . make it possible to combine regard for one's own identity with understanding of others and respect for diversity. Fundamental in this respect is the responsibility of education. . . . Education has a particular role to play in building a more united and peaceful world. It can help to affirm that integral humanism, open to life's ethical and religious dimension, which appreciates the importance of understanding and showing esteem for other cultures and the spiritual values present in them.

Catholic schools, because they are "open to life's ethical and religious dimension," are well suited to take up the task that the pope describes—a task essential to overcoming the present global hostility. This task of education is essential for what the pope writes next.

In concluding his message, John Paul II makes a special appeal to youth, who he says are "humanity's future and living stones in the building of the civilization of love."

> Dear young people of every language and culture, a high and exhilarating task awaits you: that of becoming men and women capable of solidarity, peace and love of life, with respect for everyone. Become craftsmen of a new humanity, where brothers and sisters—members all of the same family—are able at last to live in peace.

And the pope had words especially for Christian youth: "The Gospel calls you to rebuild the original unity of the human family, which has its source in God the Father, Son and Holy Spirit." This "original unity" of the human family finds its foundation in the loving communion of the Trinity. It is a "family" because it, too, reflects the "structure of love" that the Creator has designed in his creation, and because of this, the pope's admonition is not just poetry but a call that reaches to the most profound reality of human life.

SUGGESTIONS FOR CONTEMPLATION AND ACTION

1. Think of a person you do not like, or with whom you are having some difficulties. Ask yourself honestly, "Do I realize that this person has just as much worth as I do, no more and no less?" Be extremely honest with yourself about your answer.

2. Make a commitment to yourself that every day for the next week, you will consciously perform some loving act. It can be especially helpful if that act is unnoticed by anyone else and you don't receive any congratulation or praise for it.

3. Sit quietly for a certain amount of time—say five to fifteen minutes, preferably at a time of prayer and contemplation—and allow yourself to receive the love of God. What do you experience?

4. Pay attention to any occasions when you are receiving help from another person. Do you allow yourself to receive it fully, or do you try to push it away?

5. Pay attention to any occasions when you are giving help to another person. Are you giving fully and generously, or do you find yourself trying to get something out of it?

6. If you have children, ask yourself what you do to educate them in your faith. Does the education that they are receiving reflect your own values and beliefs? If not, consider how you might introduce more of your values into their education.

4

A Dignity That Brings Demands

In 1964, a year before the conclusion of the Second Vatican Council and its promulgation of *Gaudium et Spes*, the Nobel Prize committee announced a distinguished, if contradictory, set of winners. Whether intending to or not, the committee had identified two powerful and influential movements taking place in the West. One winner marked a continued trend of turning away from religion and religious morality that was gaining influence in Europe. The other marked the continuation of a strong religious tradition in the United States that sought to transform culture according to its own sensibility and moral view of society. Jean-Paul Sartre—author and philosopher—was offered the prize in literature "for his work which, rich in ideas and filled with the spirit of freedom and the quest for truth, has exerted a far-reaching influence on our age." Sartre had advanced in brilliant style the philosophy of existentialism—that man creates himself through his own actions without reference to any universal, unchanging moral law. His books, beginning with *Nausea* and including *Being and Nothingness*, The Roads to Freedom trilogy, *The Wall*, and *Existentialism Is a Humanism* were tremendously popular in both Europe and the United States. Ironically, this French intellectual embraced by the political Left had breathed new life into the legacy of the German philosophical icon of the Nazis: Friedrich

Nietzsche—at least in regard to how Sartre had advanced the rejection of Christianity, Christian morality, and indeed *any* traditional criteria for judging moral conduct. The French writer Bernard-Henri Lévy has called Sartre the "philosopher of the twentieth century," explaining that it is difficult to overestimate his influence following World War II. Lévy describes Sartre as the "prince of the younger generation that would draw from his books its mottoes, its faith, its penchant for breaking taboos and conformist dogmas, its sense that thought can become life"; and because of Sartre, this generation "was seeing things, the world, beings in it, as if for the very first time."[1]

In quite a different light, Martin Luther King Jr. was awarded the Nobel Peace Prize, for being "the first person in the Western world to have shown us that a struggle can be waged without violence . . . the first to make the message of brotherly love a reality in the course of his struggle, and he brought this message to all men, to all nations and races."[2] Dr. King brought the world a Gospel of hope epitomized by his refrain "I have a dream" during the 1963 March on Washington. The Nobel Prize committee correctly noted the universality of his message. That universality as well as the annual celebration of his civil rights accomplishments through a national holiday in the United States have tended to obscure the religious foundation of his work, even to the extent of customarily referring to him as Dr. King rather than as *Reverend* King. But within the United States, Dr. King was part of a strong reemergence of evangelical Protestantism—a movement that traced its roots through the abolitionist movement of the American Civil War back to the efforts of William Wilberforce to outlaw the slave trade in England earlier in the nineteenth century. During the 1950s, Dr. King had grown close to the guiding light of evangelicalism in America, Reverend Billy Graham, and had been invited to pray with Graham during Graham's Madison Square Garden crusade in 1957. Graham was one of the few whites close enough to King to call him by his birth name, Mike.

And there was even hope that their cooperation would one day result in a Graham and King Crusade.[3]

Despite the fact that both Sartre and King were now Nobel Prize winners, the dichotomy between the thought of these two men could hardly be greater. Sartre's philosophy was premised on the idea that there is no absolute, moral reference point for human action. Religion, for Sartre, marked a great restriction on human freedom, and in making this claim, Sartre recalled a French tradition with roots deep in the Enlightenment and its Revolution of 1789. To the contrary, Reverend King would recall time and time again St. Paul's argument at the Areopagus that we are all children of the same God and therefore are called to brotherhood and equality. King also was a champion of freedom, and he appealed to the best in the American tradition as he concluded his address on the steps of the Lincoln Memorial during the March on Washington: "When we allow freedom to ring . . . we will be able to speed up that day when all of God's children— black men and white men, Jews and Gentiles, Catholics and Protestants—will be able to join hands and to sing in the words of the old Negro spiritual, 'Free at last, free at last; thank God Almighty, we are free at last.'"

Thus Sartre and King in a way marked the polarities and the common ground of their age. They might, at this point in history, serve as a way of understanding the challenge faced by the Catholic bishops meeting during that same time in the Second Vatican Council. Both Sartre and King presented a challenge to the Catholic Church. Both men sought profound changes in Western culture. Both men premised that change as necessary to restore freedom and respect for dignity of the individual. Both men were leaders of traditions—secularism and Protestantism—that had historically represented great challenges to Catholicism. How then would the Council Fathers respond?

The response of the Council was indeed decisive to the future of Catholicism in both Europe and America. Pope Paul VI summarized the work of the Second Vatican Council as declaring a "new humanism"—a Christian humanism—by which the pope asserted "we, more than any others, honor humankind." He said that in the Second Vatican Council the Church declared itself "entirely on the side of man and in its service."[4] In *Gaudium et Spes,* the Council sought explicitly to contrast Catholicism with secularism. It stated that the world was presented with a choice between the "religion of man who makes himself God" and that of a new Christian humanism: of the "religion of God who became man."[5] At the same time, it asserted that Catholicism, too, would seek the transformation of culture in the West. The Council sought to offer a renewed focus on the practical implications of human dignity, especially as illustrated in our creation and our baptism into Christ. Pope John Paul II explored this further in his Apostolic Exhortation on the lay faithful, saying, "The dignity as a Christian, the source of equality for all members of the church, guarantees and fosters the spirit of communion and fellowship, and, at the same time, becomes the hidden dynamic force in the lay faithful's apostolate and mission. It is a dignity, however, which brings demands, the dignity of laborers called by the Lord to work in his vineyard."[6] This vineyard could no longer be considered only as the Catholic community closed in upon itself (indeed, if it ever was), but the vineyard consisted of the entire society.

This new Christian humanism found that the laity's role was essential. It emphasized the layperson's vocation to seek "the Kingdom of God by engaging in temporal affairs and by ordering them according to the plan of God."[7] Through baptism, all Christians are identified with a special character that "is not only an anthropological and sociological reality, but in a specific way, a theological and ecclesiological reality."[8] In other words, each layman and laywoman has a vocation that is not only secular, but religious as well.

In particular, the role of the laity "must be understood in light of the act of God the creator and redeemer, who has handed over the world to women and men, so that they may participate in the work of creation."⁹ Every baptized Christian has been "handed over the world." But we are to treat it as does its creator and re-deemer, that is, lovingly. The vocation of the laity is inseparable from the Lord's act of creation and redemption, and therefore this vocation is itself a participation in the activity of the God who is love.

By drawing closer to the Lord in this way, we come to under-stand our humanity: "Through work man not only transforms nature, adapting it to his own needs, but he also achieves fulfill-ment as a human being and indeed in a sense becomes 'more a human being'."¹⁰ In saying this, John Paul II sought to link the dignity of the person with a new respect for the dignity of work as well as the dignity of nature that is to be transformed by human work. Work is a gift given to humans that allows them to fulfill their vocations.

The laity is also called to a central role in the work of evangeli-zation—each baptized person's communion with Christ leads to mission, and that mission is directed toward bringing others into communion. Consequently, the laity deals most closely with the identification of Christ in each individual—in radiating the pres-ence of Christ through their love for others and in seeing the face of Christ in those they encounter in the practical reality of day-to-day living. Benedict XVI reflects upon these two aspects as they are found in true humanism, saying that it "acknowledges that man is made in the image of God and wants to help him to live in a way consonant with that dignity."¹¹

In one of his last visits to the United States, Pope John Paul encouraged our country to look beyond our borders for ways to help people. Today, charitable giving, even life-changing gifts of charity, has never seemed easier or quicker. Fighting hunger, schooling orphans, healing infirmity—we can give to almost any cause through the mail or by the Internet or even by payroll de-duction at work. Ironically, we can now help many people without

ever personally interacting with a single person. Monetary contributions make a tremendous difference, but as important—and
indeed indispensable—as monetary contributions are for the success of charities, I want to focus on another facet of America's
giving habits: the twenty billion hours, or about sixty-six hours
per person, given every year in volunteering. What drives people
to spend their time—which could be spent on themselves, or in
the workplace—working for other people, often with other
people, without repayment? What motivates the Christian to
engage in service, in giving of self?

Certainly, many things motivate people to give. Some give in
the hope of reciprocity or other personal benefits such as public
recognition or tax benefits. The philosopher Thomas Hobbes
degraded the idea motivating charity as, in reality, only reflecting
man's self-centeredness. "Grief for the calamity of another is Pity,
and arises from the imagination that the like calamity may befall
himself," wrote Hobbes.[12] However, his attempt to convert Christian altruism represented by "do unto others as you would have
them do unto you"[13] into really meaning "so that they will do
similarly unto you" fails to convince. There are just too many who
give of themselves without such thoughts.

The golden rule of "do unto others" was placed in concrete
imagery by Christ in the parable of the Good Samaritan. The
parable emphasizes the importance of a personal encounter in
the work of charity. Scripture recounts a subtle difference in the
language used to describe the encounter between the victim and
those who pass him by or stay to help. Each of these travelers approaches the man lying beaten differently before each is faced
with the decision to stay or leave. The priest saw him, but passed
by. The Levite came near "the place" and passed by. The Samaritan, in contrast, came near "him" and had compassion. It is when
someone approaches and in coming "near him" engages in a personal encounter that the plight of the victim in suffering moves
the other to compassion.[14]

But the Christian is under a new and unique obligation. This encounter is even more radical: "in everyone we can and must recognize the countenance of Christ the Son of Man, especially when tears and sorrows make it plain to see."[15] In saying this at the close of the Second Vatican Council, Paul VI was calling the laity especially to a higher involvement in their work to renew society. If we see Christ in the suffering of all those around us, then our only response is a response of love. This response has as its essential element a loving communion between the two—a communion that forms a living stone in the building up of the civilization of love.

In *Deus Caritas Est,* Pope Benedict reminds us that, "My deep personal sharing in the needs and sufferings of others becomes a sharing of my very self with them. . . . I must give to others not only something that is my own, but my very self; I must be personally present in my gift."[16] This is an essential aspect of the Christian's work of charity. In the Christian understanding of a loving communion there is always present the idea of gift of self. Indeed, all Christian charity as expressed in these words of the pope take as its source the gift that Christ makes of himself in the Eucharist.

I would like to focus on some examples of people who live out the vocation to love in this active way set out and renewed in the Council—to examine the means they employ, the love of God that propels them, the selflessness that enables them to expend themselves for others, and the fulfillment that draws them to this work and rewards it. These are people who have recognized in another person's humanity and misfortunes the symmetry and asymmetry that enable love.

Dan and Cubby Lahood have kept their doors open to children who are severely challenged mentally and physically, providing care and companionship during the day for them. The struggles of this couple to bring aid to families with children who have disabilities are exhausting and yet so rewarding for them.

Some would consider the responsibilities placed on the couple to be limiting and the burden of such care to be, at times, unbearable. But they consider it otherwise. They describe their life now as follows:

> The sense of freedom that we've experienced since we've undertaken our ministry and tried through difficult times, happy times, times of great challenge to conform to God's will, is the most freeing, most liberating, most satisfying—words fail. But what it makes us feel is more human. We cry real tears, our laughs are genuine. We can appreciate the beauty of life even among the thorns that surround us.[17]

This joy and consolation comes to so many through what the Lahoods call their "ministry"; it gives depth and meaning to humanity. It is not so much because they achieve "great" things, but because they do "small things with great love."[18] Gift of self means everything we are given—every talent—is given as a gift. Every moment is a chance and opportunity for conveying love. Says Dan, "We can't do it like he [Jesus] did, we can't raise anyone from the dead, we can't make somebody walk, but if they can't walk, we can lift them, if they can't put a spoon in their mouths we can feed them."[19] If in baptism we become part of the Body of Christ, and if Christ has no hands but ours in this world, how can we keep those hands in our pockets?

Thirty years ago, four councils of the Knights of Columbus in Cedar Rapids that had contributed to the welfare of people with intellectual disabilities through raising money realized that the real need was for more housing for those people. What began as an isolated search for a single house led to a nonprofit organization with twenty houses serving over ninety residents with developmental disabilities. What they created was a resource that not only improved lives by offering housing, but fostered an integration of those lives into the entire community—their own community—enabling those in need to continue their lives and relationships.

Their work shows a great connection with the vocation of love, especially through the secular calling of the laity to work toward a just ordering of society, not merely contributing to the improvement of individual lives. This is not simply another example of "doing good"; rather, it reflects how in one way the laity is able to reflect and project the love of Christ—an aspect of the love of Christ that again is found and expressed three times in the baptismal rite: inclusion in the community of the faithful. Paul VI took up this context of each person—the inclusion through love—in an address the day after the conclusion of the Council: "'Communion' speaks of a double, life-giving participation: the incorporation of Christians into the life of Christ, and the communication of that life of charity to the entire body of the Faithful, in this world and in the next, union with Christ and in Christ, and union among Christians, in the Church."[20]

Members of the lay faithful "can never remain in isolation from the community, but must live in a continual interaction with others, with a lively sense of fellowship, rejoicing in an equal dignity and common commitment to bring to fruition the immense treasure that each has inherited."[21] Thus community is needed intrinsically by every person, not just needed by those who are in misfortune.

It is just such recognition of the reciprocal and necessary nature of communion that is found in Travis County Jail in Texas—particularly on the second and fourth Thursdays of each month. Built in the shadow of the courthouse, the facility deals with all levels of inmates—inmates who in their various ways had disrupted the order of justice and dignity. And yet it is precisely here, where isolation and separation abound, that four men and others uncounted have been living and working at keeping solidarity and communion alive. To many, both religious and nonreligious alike, there would seem little reason for an octogenarian

like Gene Raulie to visit those in prison, and yet in his visits to
pray with inmates, he has tapped into the essence of the vocation
to love—a vocation that can be lived out anywhere, from either
side of a prison wall. Their praying together is not proselytizing.
Rather, in praying the same prayers that millions pray throughout
the world, they proclaim in a personal, and we might even say intimate, way the unity of the church. In prayer, all dwell in Christ,
and through Christ, all are once again able to exist as they were
created: as equals.[22]

For some time now, the Knights of Columbus has been partici-
pating in an international project through the Wheelchair Foundation. Counting those who donate, assemble and contract,
collect and distribute, and finally receive, thousands of people
participate in the process start to finish. The concept is simple:
for seventy-five dollars, you can buy a wheelchair for someone
who can't afford one, thus providing mobility for that person. I
was in Mexico for one of the wheelchair distributions and had the
privilege of working with the volunteers. When simply donating
money, you'll find it difficult to imagine the impact your sacrifice
can have in another's life. You might also underestimate the
impact their change in life can have on you. Going into a situation like that, you might expect the day to blur into a flipbook of
difficulties and maladies, and yet coming away, the feeling is precisely the opposite—the buzzing of hope in a town square full of
people and families. We could see people who, for the first time,
could go places rather than be carried. Having hope brings joy.
Giving hope brings joy. That hope and joy could be seen in every
person present—in the love of the families who had carried and
cared for a child or a parent for so long and even in those who
were alone in the world, forced to test the strength of the community. Some donors had to scrimp to sponsor one wheelchair,
while others gave many. But for everyone who participated, seeing
the faces of those who were to be helped, even before they re-

ceived the gift, made the volunteers realize giving a wheelchair was an inexpensive way to change a life in a dramatic way.

One girl named Funy wrote a letter to the Knights of Columbus and gave it to me that day. It was filled with her joy and gratitude, with not a word about her own difficulties and not even mentioning the gift itself. She was grateful for "having met such 'precious treasures,' my friends," saying, "I found my angel in you." She ended the letter with, "For me you are not just knights. You are my angels." In the moment of supporting someone so different from you and yet having an enormous ability to love, without holding on to "self-respect" or pride, one realizes how enormous it is to be human: the greatness of each human person.

In so many guises, in difficulties, yet still the human person waits for love. And through love, through reaching out, we can come together to work for the same goal. As my wife, Dorian, and I lifted Funy into her chair, we gave her a new mobility, but she gave us something more: love and joy and a better understanding of what it means to be human. I can only hope that by our gift she felt we were proclaiming that human life is more precious to us than material goods, and that her life, her joy, her love are precious. A small donation had changed her life and ours as well. During the last several years the Knights of Columbus has distributed more than twelve thousand wheelchairs—each in its own way a building block in the civilization of love.

I have kept a copy of Funy's letter, and I often think of her words, "You are my angels." To be an angel for seventy-five dollars is not an opportunity that comes along every day. But in a way it does. Most of the world today lives in conditions in which seventy-five dollars or even much less can change a person's life or that of an entire family.

Today the parable told by Jesus of the rich man and Lazarus is being lived out on a global scale. St. Luke recounts the story: "There was a rich man, who was dressed in purple and fine linen and who feasted sumptuously every day. And at his gate lay a poor man named Lazarus ... who longed to satisfy his hunger with what fell from the rich man's table." The poor man died and "was carried away by the angels" while the rich man, when he died, was tormented in Hades. Finally, the rich man cried out, "Have mercy on me, and send Lazarus to dip the tip of his finger in water and cool my tongue; for I am in agony." But the rich man is told that this is impossible because "between you and us a great chasm has been fixed, so that those who might want to pass from here to you cannot do so."[23]

While seventy-five dollars is quite a bit more than the value of the crumbs that fall from the average American's dinner table, it is only about the price of dinner for two and a movie or two tickets to a major-league baseball game or a full tank of gas for the family SUV. In other words, it is an amount easily within reach of the average American. And yet for millions in the world it is an enormous sum of money. But the chasm that exists between us and those in desperate poverty is not as great as that which Jesus described in the parable: The chasm that separates us can be crossed.

Yet there are struggles and times when that angelic feeling or that "helper's high" that characterizes those who give in a personal way may be lost. On a number of occasions during the last three decades, I had the privilege of being with Mother Teresa of Calcutta. Perhaps more than any other person of our age, Mother Teresa impressed upon the world the reality that it is possible to give of one's self to the "poorest of the poor" for an entire lifetime. It is not an exaggeration to say that Mother Teresa became for an entire generation an icon of selfless charity. She crossed that chasm every day. As she would say when we met, "Take time to love Jesus in the poor."

Like many others who spent even brief moments with Mother Teresa, I was astonished to read in the newly published collection of her writings, *Come Be My Light*, that Mother Teresa herself experienced no spiritual consolation through the last decades of her ministry. She lived for many years in a sort of "dark night of the soul."[24] Those who personally encountered her joy and her happiness find it almost impossible to believe that she would write:

> Please pray for me—the longing for God is terribly painful and yet the darkness is becoming greater. What contradiction there is in my soul.—The pain within is so great—that I really don't feel anything for all the publicity and the talk of the people. Please ask Our Lady to be my Mother in this darkness.[25]

And yet throughout her ministry she persevered and did not begrudge her work. She often stated the reason for her charity, the ultimate reason, which, although sounding to some ears as too emotionless to count as love, nevertheless is the true and only unassailable reason for love—her relationship with God. For in the end, "good feelings" cannot be promised, but the absence of such feelings does not diminish the joy, love, or achievement that comes from acts of charity. Just as depression and other disturbances do not alter reality but alter only the perception of reality, so Mother Teresa's dark night of the soul did not affect the reality of what she achieved in helping millions of the poor or what she sought: union with Christ, through love.

Fundamentally, one of the only ways in which we can show our love for God physically is through service to him through people. Through the face of the unfortunate, Christ provides himself to us, as an opportunity for showing our love. Our service of love is what enables Christ to speak to us—not only in how it physically brings us in contact with the poor but also and especially because it conditions us to receive and welcome his words. It takes humility and love on our part to listen to Christ. It is not easy to listen to the words right before the parable of the Good Samaritan, when Christ praises the Father because "although you have hidden these things from the wise and the learned you have revealed them to the childlike."[26]

What we can hear and learn, what we can be taught, is what it means to be human, what it means to love. Mother Teresa would often remark on the great dignity of the poor and even of their charity to one another. "The poor give us much more than we give them. They're such strong people, living day to day with no food. And they never curse, never complain. We don't have to give them pity or sympathy. We have so much to learn from them."[27] Benedict XVI, in *Deus Caritas Est,* noted that service to those in need is at the same time an act preparing us for the encounter with Christ: "Only my readiness to encounter my neighbor and to show him love makes me sensitive to God as well. Only if I serve my neighbor can my eyes be opened to what God does for me and how much he loves me."[28] Thus, in a different way, self-giving leads to self-discovery.

For so many who have experienced the joy and fulfillment of the service of love, it can be difficult to understand why others do not pursue it. In a lecture at the Institute for the Psychological Sciences on "The Role of Theatre in the Evangelization of Culture," priest and playwright Fr. Peter Cameron explored the need for thought-provoking theater in our times: "One main reason why the human being lives bereft of the meaning of life is because he has nothing to inspire him to search the depths of his self so as to discover the truth of his human 'I.'" Confronting our existence, he suggests, brings us face to face with three truths we did not cause and cannot fulfill ourselves: our creation, our certain desires infinite in scope, and our expectation of happiness and fulfillment.[29]

Ultimately, these truths lead us to comprehend God's love more fully and to accept that our need for the service of love is to be found in our created nature and our need for redemption. The Second Vatican Council, in the moment of its "greatest awareness and effectiveness,"[30] expressed a similar conclusion in a more concrete way in *Gaudium et Spes*: "Man can fully discover his true self only in a sincere giving of himself."[31] This implies that something in the act of self-giving reveals or causes us to realize our true nature. More important, it is a promise—self-giving is not simply an act of the *looking* for self but an act of the *discovery* of self. In every Good Samaritan situation, then, there is the invitation to give oneself and discover anew one's true self: a being created out of love, in the image of a triune God, oriented toward others, with a great capacity for love and, therefore, a great capacity for joy.

John Paul II suggested that our ordering of creation cannot be separated from the circumstances of our creation in the image of the Trinitarian God. Man, as a being created by "the divine Artist" is like a work of art by which "artists express themselves to the point where their work becomes a unique disclosure of their own being."[33] Our being in the likeness of God is manifest in how we, like the Trinity, are oriented toward others in family and in community for love, and how our relationships with others are defined by and reflect the persons of the Trinity.

Most Christians have heard how baptism calls one to be the "light of Christ," or how we must recognize the face of Christ in others. Fewer, however, recognize how the Holy Spirit is reflected in or "radiates" through our relationships. However, John Paul suggests that a sincere giving of self is accepting fully each person's creation in the image of the Trinitarian God. Some stumble on this recognition of the human person in reference to another being. We tend to think of "self" as being something that is defined and designed according to our own specifications or that to be a mature person is to accept autonomy and even solitude. It can be difficult then to accept self-giving, which can seem extreme and even tend to destroy self rather than realize it.

In *Radiation of Fatherhood*,[34] John Paul II voiced the struggle of giving up self to accept the presence of God in our relationships with others. This play, published under his nom de plume, Andrzej Jawien, when he was still a priest in Poland, gives us an insight into the phrase in *Gaudium et Spes*. From a dramatic perspective, the play is unconventional, being less a dialogue between characters and more a dialogue between minds and souls. Yet, because of this very fact, it is suited to its subject: the interior struggles of love and religion.

The main character, Adam, is father to Monica—and a fairly good one. He talks with her, he looks at a family photo album with her, walks with her in the woods; yet through the dialogues, he cannot recognize that the capacity for love cannot come from himself, but only from God. Both Monica and the woman, Mother, plead with him to open himself to the fact that through his fatherhood, the paternity of God the Father is present to his children, and that likewise his presence will be always present in his children. He hesitates and questions himself:

All this I know. But is it enough to know? I choose loneliness to remain myself and nobody else. This is what my world is created from. Do I really remain myself?"[35]

The dialogue is poignant and, like the play itself, mostly unresolved, with Adam wanting more and more to draw closer to his daughter yet unwilling to truly give himself. Instead, he battles between enjoying the self-oriented, self-imposed loneliness and needing—and being needed for—the love that would lead him to union with others.

This ultimate gift of self, in which the service of love is the result of our radiation of God's love to others, can be seen in the works of those around us: when service is most effective, when love most true, each reflects divine love. For this reason, active or visible service of love is fundamental to giving of self: "Following the example given in the parable of the Good Samaritan, Christian charity is first of all the simple response to immediate needs and specific situations."[36] The fullness of self-giving is not realized by only giving what one *has* but what one *is* as well.

Martin Luther King Jr., the day before his assassination, spoke about the parable of the Good Samaritan. And like everybody else, he had his own interpretation. He talked about a trip he made on the road from Jerusalem to Jericho on which the parable is set, when he realized something about the parable's location. It is a steep, "winding, meandering road, . . . really conducive for ambushing." Suddenly, he doesn't condemn the priest and the Levite for not stopping but makes excuses for them. It is, after all, "a dangerous road," on which anything could happen. Perhaps they "looked over that man on the ground and wondered if robbers were still around. Or it's possible that they felt that the man on the ground was merely faking. And he was acting like he had been robbed and hurt, in order to seize them over there, lure them there for quick and easy seizure. And so the first question that the Levite asked was, 'If I stop to help this man, what will happen to me?' Thus besides compassion, it took courage for the Samaritan to stop. It took an initial step away from focusing on oneself in order to recognize the person before him, the person who could be within reach if he only reached out. But then the Good Samaritan came by. And he reversed the question: 'If I do not stop to help this man, what will happen to him?'"[37]

Contrary to Hobbes's self-centered characterization of compassion as resulting from a desire to ease the discomfort of imagining oneself in the other's place, Martin Luther King Jr.'s version of love incorporates a willingness to switch places with the other, if necessary—to join and share the suffering, or greater suffering, for the sake of the other person. Because love is a complete expending of self—because, even though there are many rewards, love gives without expectation or contingency of reciprocation—it takes a huge act of faith and courage to act on love.

Ultimately, we see in the parable of the Good Samaritan the Lord himself. Christ had the courage to stop and help a suffering humanity. Christ as well had the courage to accept suffering and death for the sake of that suffering humanity.

When the people of the Nobel committee awarded the prize for literature to Jean-Paul Sartre, they were recognizing more than just a brilliant man of letters. In a way they were also recognizing the cultural ascendancy of a way of living and of viewing the world in which there is no constant reference point for judging human action or for understanding human suffering. But for the Christian, there is just such a constant reference point to understand all aspects of the human condition, including the morality of human action and even human suffering. And that reference point is the love of God incarnated in the person of Jesus Christ. This is the measure by which all things human may be evaluated and seen in true perspective. And this was a fundamental work of the Second Vatican Council, to present this reality of Jesus before the world and to renew his church, as Paul VI stated, as the church of the Good Samaritan.

Some years ago I had the opportunity to visit Mexico City for a conference on international law where I was to deliver a paper on religious liberty. On my way to the meeting each day, I walked across the enormous downtown plaza of the Zócalo and then passed along the side of the magnificent Baroque-style cathedral. Sitting alongside the wall of the cathedral every morning were dozens of men sitting two or three feet apart, resting their backs against the cathedral wall and each holding a handwritten sign reading "plumber," "carpenter," or "laborer," among other professions. Many held small bags of tools. All were hoping for a job that day. Every so often someone would walk up to one of the men, a brief discussion would occur, and then both would leave together. It was possible even in those brief moments to perceive in those men the dignity of the laborer who has been called.

At the heart of the "dignity" of the Christian about which the Council spoke is the *privilege* of believing in Jesus Christ. Why this privilege has been given by grace to some and not to others is a mystery. But this dignity and this privilege have lifted each Christian out of a human condition in modern society that Jean-Paul

Sartre had described with the single word: "nausea." This dignity and this privilege remains even during times of suffering or during a "dark night of the soul," as Mother Teresa's example testified. But, as the Council reminds us, "It is a dignity, however, which brings demands, the dignity of laborers called by the Lord to work in his vineyard."

SUGGESTIONS FOR CONTEMPLATION AND ACTION

1. Think of an act of charity that a person you know needs. Why hasn't anyone performed this act for that person? Why haven't you performed this act? Consider barriers that you or the other person may have put up.

2. Make a list of your talents. Be conscious of how you use those talents throughout that day. How, when, and for whom do you use them?

3. Think of someone you encounter briefly in a utilitarian setting: the train conductor, the person at the cash register, etc. Consider how this moment of interaction—however brief, however mundane—has been given to you both, to be shared by you both. Consider how many actions have been performed in order to give you both this opportunity to stand as a reflection of God's love for the other person. Consider also how you might treat this person differently if you thought he or she had a different position—a celebrity's personal manager, a stockbroker retiree, etc. How can you treat each the same, with the same investment in the other person? It can be as simple as a genuine smile—a smile that doesn't seek to express your happiness but rather seeks to pass it on.

5

The Domestic Church

We have discussed how being made in the image of God—the *imago dei*—is seen and practiced in service of others. In a special way, it is found uniquely within marriage and the family—the first context of persons mentioned in Genesis: "And He said 'Let us make man in our own image.'. . . So God created man in his own image, in the image of God he created him; male and female he created them."[1] Yet in order to understand love in the family, it is helpful to first examine the "our" of "in our own image"—the Trinity. "It is the doctrine of the *imago Dei* that decides the destiny of all theology," said theologian Emil Brunner.[2] But what does this really mean for us?

The mystery of the Trinity is perhaps the most profound and difficult for human minds to understand. One legend says that St. Augustine was contemplating this doctrine one day when he was walking along the shore. He saw a small child take water out of the sea with a shell and pour it into a small hole in the sand. Augustine asked the child what he was doing. The child said, "I'm emptying the sea into this hole."

"But you'll never be able to fit the whole sea into that hole," said Augustine.

The child, who was really an angel, replied, "No more will you be able to understand the mystery of the Trinity."

Nevertheless, Augustine went on to complete his treatise *De Trinitate* ("On the Trinity," written between A.D. 400 and 420), now long considered the classic work on this mystery.[3] For Augustine, human beings resemble the Trinity principally in the different aspects of the mind. Examining the nature of thought, he divides it into memory, understanding, and will (or love).[4] "Here we are then with the mind remembering itself, understanding itself, loving itself," he writes. "If we see this we see a trinity, not yet God of course, but already the image of God."[5] For Augustine, the human being as a rational creature is the image of God.

Augustine's view sounded the keynote for the discussion for many centuries. Yet John Paul II made a revolutionary change in the discussion with his proposal that human beings resemble the Trinity in our *inter*personal relationships as well as *intra*personal relationships. In his 1994 *Letter to Families*, John Paul II wrote, "In the light of the New Testament it is possible to discern how the primordial model of the family is to be sought in God himself, in the Trinitarian mystery of his life. The divine 'We' is the eternal pattern of the human 'we', especially of that 'we' formed by the man and the woman created in the divine image and likeness."[6]

Angelo Cardinal Scola, the patriarch of Venice, suggests that while the classic doctrine of the *imago Dei* formulated by St. Augustine cannot be ignored, the human person must also be "considered in his entirety," that is, "insofar as he is created from the beginning as man and woman."[7] If this is so, it automatically takes us to marriage and the family. Not only is the family almost always the locus of a person's most important relationships, but the family metaphor has been built into the language of Christian doctrine, which, after all, speaks of a Father and a Son.

This idea has been frequently echoed in Christian literature and art. After the death of the Dutch artist Rembrandt in 1669, officials found in his studio a painting they considered unfinished. Titled *The Return of the Prodigal Son,* it remains one of his greatest masterpieces.

As is well known, the prodigal son (see Luke 15:11–32) insisted upon his inheritance early and embarked on a way of life that could only be seen as a total repudiation of his family's values. His isolation from them is complete when, by his own recklessness, he is driven into poverty.

The painting depicts the moment when the son returns, kneels before his father, and embraces him. His father returns the embrace, his hands on his son's shoulders, drawing him still closer to himself. The father's eyes are closed, but it is obvious that he now sees his son in a way that transcends what is merely visible. The father's face is bathed in light, a sign of the grace that has brought him and his son to this moment. There is no smile on his face. His own suffering and that which he now sees in his son's condition are too profound.

Rembrandt depicts the father wearing a red mantle, traditionally a symbol of the Lord's glory. This image reminds us what the Church Fathers taught: the glory of the Lord is man redeemed. The son is redeemed by his return. The father, too, finds redemption in his willingness to accept the son's return. Thus the grace of God the Father is sufficient to reconcile father and son and to heal the family.

The parable of the Prodigal Son places one petition of the Lord's Prayer within the context of the family: "Our Father ... forgive us our trespasses as we forgive those who trespass against us." Rembrandt has painted the prodigal son in such a way that he represents Everyman kneeling repentant before the Father.

Love implies both a *self* and an *other*, one who loves and the one who is loved—figuratively, a Father and a Son. This self and this other must have some point of contact that connects them. This point of contact, this means of connection, is nothing other than love. Love can be equated with the Holy Spirit, who, in the language of the creed, "proceeds from the Father and the Son." It is in this way that conjugal love mirrors the love of the Trinity. In his recent book, *Divine Likeness*, Marc Cardinal Ouellet, archbishop of Quebec, writes:

> The Father is the original gift whose fruit is the Son. The Son is fecund together with the Father in spirating the Holy Spirit as the fruit of their reciprocal Love. By contrast, the Holy Spirit is not the origin of another Person, but seals the unity of the Father and the Son in himself, as Person-Gift.[8]

Similarly, Ouellet points out that the dynamic of love moves from "I" to "Thou" to "We": "The reciprocal gift of the man and woman in faith first and foremost generates the couple as such, which is already a 'third' in respect to the two individuals who constitute it."[9]

These insights resemble those of the classic work *I and Thou* by the twentieth-century philosopher Martin Buber, who said that any genuine relationship moves from an "I-it" polarity to a relationship of "I-Thou." At first, we may see the other person simply as an object, a means of gratifying our needs and desires. Developmental psychologists tell us that infants begin by thinking this way. At some point, however, we realize that the other is a living subject, an "I" like oneself. In other words, the "it" becomes a "Thou." It is only here between an "I" and a "Thou" that a true relationship, a true love, can begin.

As John Paul II writes, "Being a person in the image and likeness of God thus also involves existing in a relationship, in relation to the other 'I.' This is a prelude to the definitive self-revelation of the triune God: a living unity in the communion of the Father, Son, and Holy Spirit."[10] Thus, in this Christian understanding of the I-Thou relationship, each person is called to communion—a special one that reflects that communion of love existing within the Trinity. But John Paul II sees this communion as even more particular: this communion has a special form because God has created humanity as male and female. Because the human person is created male and female, the vocation to love, which is each person's calling, has a special form, and that form is revealed most clearly in the marriage relationship. Christian marriage therefore is a primary way in which we find revealed God's plan for humanity to participate in the expressive love of Trinitarian communion.

Ouellet speaks of three stages in the growth of marital love. The first "marks the passage from being in love to really loving the person. Being in love always carries an element of illusion and the projection of one's own I. It is not exempt from a hidden egoism that emerges from the circumstances." One could add that this egoism stems precisely from viewing the other as a kind of "it," a means of gratifying certain desires and achieving certain objectives, some of them innocent in themselves, some of them no doubt less so. Genuine love, on the other hand, "accepts the other as she is, and not as the ideal person he would like her to be."[11]

The transition between love for the other as an "it," a mere compendium of desirable qualities, to a "Thou" is beautifully expressed by the nineteenth-century English poet Elizabeth Barrett Browning, whose own marriage with Robert Browning offers one of the most sublime examples of marital love in literary history.

> If thou must love me, let it be for naught
> Except for love's sake only. Do not say,
> "I love her for her smile—her look—her way
> Of speaking gently. . . .
> For these things in themselves, Belovèd, may
> Be changed, or change for thee—and love, so wrought,
> May be unwrought so. . . .
> But love me for love's sake, that evermore
> Thou mayst love on, through love's eternity.[12]

The second phase of marital love, according to Ouellet, is the transformation of love to charity. What began as romantic love between a man and a woman grows into a type of the love expressed by Christ for his bride, the church. "Little by little, the charity of Christ becomes the 'form' of their love, with its characteristics of pure gratuity, proven fidelity, and perpetuity."[13] In this way Christ enters into the fabric and substance of the couple's love for each other. This is the meaning of St. Paul's hymn to love in his First Letter to the Corinthians: "Love is patient; love is kind; love is not envious or boastful or arrogant or rude. . . . It bears all things, believes all things, hopes all things, endures all things. Love never ends."[14] Thus, Christ's love becomes the form of married love.

Finally love undergoes its third metamorphosis, and here, too, we see a reflection of the Trinity and another sense in which man and woman are the image and likeness of God. God is creative; God causes new life to come into existence. A man and a woman joined in the sacred bond of marriage have the same privilege and responsibility. Ouellet speaks of "the spiritual and physical fecundity of love."[15] In bearing and raising children, a married couple reflects the creative power of God himself. In this way the family is its own culture of life and culture of love and becomes the essential building block of the civilization of love.

But children cannot be brought into the world and left to their own devices. Even if they survived, they would almost certainly be unable to reach the full potential of their humanity without the support and guidance that only a loving home can offer. Thus the creative power of the family lies not only in its "fecundity" but in its capacity to pass on the essential truths of human existence—which are the mysteries of Christianity—to the children it raises, "so that," as John Paul II has said, "family life itself becomes an itinerary of faith and in some way a Christian initiation and a school of following Christ."[16]

Today, marriage is under increased pressure, with the number of married women in the United States standing at a mere 51 percent. For every two marriages contracted in the United States in the 1990s, there was one divorce. Of all people in the United States over fifteen years of age, 20 percent have been divorced at some point. Among adults in the fifty to fifty-nine age group, the figure is approximately 40 percent.[17]

The assumption, of course, is that by divorcing, spouses will be happier by leaving an unhappy marriage. "Psychotherapeutic thinking in the 1970s and 1980s largely dismissed commitment to children as a reason for trying to 'save' a marriage. Commitment to self was all," observes Barbara Dafoe Whitehead in her book *The Divorce Culture*.[18] Sadly, spouses who buy into such reasoning will often find themselves misled. A 2002 study concluded:

> Unhappily married adults who divorced or separated were no happier, on average, than unhappily married adults who stayed married. Even unhappy spouses who had divorced and remarried were no happier, on average, than unhappy spouses who stayed married. This was true even after controlling for race, age, gender, and income.[19]

Divorce not only shatters the lives of the two spouses but also forces children to pay the consequences of their parents' actions. Both statistical and anecdotal evidence suggest that children of divorce are victims whose emotional scars linger long after their parents' marriage ends. Elizabeth Marquardt, herself a child of divorce, conducted a study of more than fifteen hundred children from divorced homes and discussed her findings in her 2005 book, *Between Two Worlds*. She wrote of such children:

> This is the truth about us: Some of us, many more than those from intact families, struggle with serious problems. Our parents' divorce is linked to our higher rates of depression, suicidal attempts and thoughts, health problems, childhood sexual abuse, school dropout, failure to attend college, arrests, addiction, teen pregnancy, and more. Some of us were practically abandoned to raise ourselves in the wake of our parents' divorce and turned to drugs or alcohol

or thrill seeking to numb our pain. Some of us were abused by new adults who came into the house when one of our parents left. Some of us continue to struggle with the scars left from our parents' divorce: we have a harder time finishing school, getting and keeping jobs, maintaining relationships, and having lasting marriages. We end up living on the margins, struggling with our pain, while our friends and neighbors move on with their lives.

Yet those who are visibly suffering are the tip of the iceberg. The others, the ones without seriously disabling problems, are everywhere—at your workplace, at school, at church. We don't look much different from anyone else. We might seem a bit more guarded, a bit slower to make new friends, a bit more anxious about life in general. But we do manage to make friends, to fall in love, accomplish goals, succeed at work. Some of us do quite well.

If you ask any of us about our lives, though, you'll discover that our parents' divorce is central to the story of our childhoods and to who we are today. We grew up too soon. We were not sure where we belonged ... we had to figure out things for ourselves—what is right and wrong, what to believe, whether there is a God. We never knew if could ask for help if we needed it. When we faced struggles, we thought it was up to us alone to make sense of it, because the silence about our childhoods seemed to leave us little other choice.[20]

This snapshot reveals just how traumatic divorce is for children. Studies have shown that children of divorce have difficulty with their own relationships, with adjusting to adulthood, and with God and religion.[21]

This combination of wounded parents and traumatized children provides a real challenge to the church at large and to those ministering as pastors of souls. Every priest and marriage counselor ought to know how destructive divorce is and how rarely it betters life even for the divorcees. Many programs exist that can help save a marriage, and these are to be commended, but other programs must be created to reach out to those who have been adversely affected by divorce. While some Catholic parishes have such programs for adult divorcees, few, if any, have programs for the children of divorce. This must change if we are to give the next generation the tools to build a culture of love.

St. Thomas Aquinas argued that the principal purpose of marriage was the "good of the offspring" and that in accomplishing this purpose, "nature intends not only the begetting of offspring, but also its education and development." Therefore, Aquinas observed that "we derive three things from our parents, namely existence, nourishment and education." Aquinas also distinguished the human family from that of other animals, such as birds who need the support of parents for a relatively short time, concluding that with the human person, "since the child needs the parents' care for a long time, there is a very great tie between male and female."[22]

In *Familiaris Consortio*, John Paul II sought to provide a more comprehensive theological understanding of the marital relationship and the responsibility of parents when he wrote:

> Being rooted in the personal and total self-giving of the couple, and being required by the good of the children, the indissolubility of marriage finds its ultimate truth in the plan that God has manifested in His revelation: He wills and He communicates the indissolubility of marriage as a fruit, a sign and a requirement of the absolutely faithful love that God has for man and that the Lord Jesus has for the Church.[23]

Here, at last, we find the love that "bears all things," and the love that "endures all things"—even to the cross. It is here that the married couple unites their love to that "love that never ends" that they may participate in "love's eternity." The Orthodox theologian Paul Evdokimov goes so far as to say, "By virtue of the sacrament of matrimony, *every couple marries Christ*."[24]

John Paul II often spoke of marriage in terms of the total gift of one's self to another person. The totality of this gift has always been understood in the Catholic tradition to include the irrevocability of the gift. If the gift can be recalled, that is, if the unity of the persons that the gift makes possible is conditioned upon the possibility that it can be dissolved, it cannot be considered total. This conditional giving then cannot mirror Christ's gift of himself to the church, which so often has been described precisely as the gift of the bridegroom to his bride.

John Paul II described St. Paul's "hymn to love" in his First Letter to the Corinthians as the *Magna Carta* of the civilization of love. He then explained that this understanding of Christlike love is the key element in building a civilization of love. "What is important," he wrote, "is not so much individual actions (whether selfish or altruistic), so much as the radical acceptance of the understanding of man as a person who 'finds himself' by making a sincere gift of self. . . . This is *the most important dimension* of the civilization of love."[25]

Another way in which the church has viewed the mystery of the "sincere gift of self" of husband and wife to each other is in the matter of their marital intimacy. Pope Paul VI in his 1968 encyclical *Humanae Vitae* ("Of Human Life") reaffirmed the church's teaching that "each and every marriage act must remain open to the transmission of life." He pointed out that the conjugal act has "two inseparable aspects: union and procreation." Birth control violates both. The fact that it impedes procreation is obvious, but how does it affect the union of the couple? Paul VI stressed that contraception risks dehumanizing the relationship between husband and wife:

It is also to be feared that the man, growing used to the employment of contraceptive practices, may finally lose respect for the woman and, no longer caring for her physical and psychological equilibrium, may come to the point of considering her as a mere instrument of selfish enjoyment and no longer as his respected and beloved companion.[26]

For Paul VI, then, contraception runs the substantial risk of retrogression in the marital relationship. "Thou" is demoted to "it."

Elaborating on Paul VI's teaching, John Paul II explains that withholding an essential part of the sexual act puts a block in the way of the "communion of persons." If marriage is characterized by the total giving of self in love to the other, contraception imposes a barrier between them; the self-giving is no longer total and unconditional. As a result, blocking the procreative nature of the spouses' physical union does violence to the union of the two persons in the marriage, which John Paul II states must always be a union "in truth and love."

"It can be said that in the case of an artificial separation of these two aspects, a real bodily union is carried out in the conjugal act, but it does not correspond to the interior truth and to the dignity of personal communion—communion of persons," John Paul II observed.[27] In his *Letter to Families*, he explained in more depth:

In the conjugal act, husband and wife are called to confirm in a responsible way the mutual gift of self which they have made to each other in the marriage covenant. The logic of the total gift of self to the other involves a potential openness to procreation: in this way the marriage is called to even greater fulfillment as a family. Certainly the mutual gift of husband and wife does not have the begetting of children as its only end, but is in itself a mutual communion of love and of life. The intimate truth of this gift must always be safeguarded.[28]

The "intimate truth" of which the pope speaks has been experienced by many married couples who have sought to live their intimate lives together while maintaining this "openness" to procreation. In doing so, they have benefited from new developments in natural family planning over the past several decades. This new method enables a couple to time their periods of intimacy to coincide precisely with infertile times in the wife's cycle. Natural family planning "differs from the old 'Rhythm' method in being based on sound scientific information which allows the woman to observe accurately the signs and symptoms of her fertility cycle."[29] Admittedly, some argue that natural methods may be less effective in preventing unwanted pregnancies than some forms of artificial birth control.[30] On the other hand, some advocates of natural family planning have found that, conservatively practiced, this method is virtually 100 percent effective and that, in any event, it avoids the serious potential consequences of chemical and barrier birth-control methods.

Natural family planning has many significant benefits of its own, and many Catholic couples say that it has blessed their marriages.[31] Some even have used it to help conceive a child after years of infertility. Married couples practicing natural family planning to avoid pregnancy often find that their mutual commitment to this approach strengthens their knowledge of and communication with each other. In a study of the psychological effects of natural family planning, Richard J. Fehring, associate professor at the Marquette University College of Nursing, found that the majority of couples using this method felt that it enhanced their sense of spiritual well-being. Fehring believes that such natural methods "can help a person be more open to the needs of one's spouse" and "more enriching to this relationship."[32]

The Christian perspective on responsible procreative decision making is based on the fact that we have not created ourselves and that our life is a gift. We all depend upon someone else for our existence, and ultimately that someone is God. All life is a gift—a gift that is a result of an expressive love that flows from the God who *is* love. Therefore we are called to live in a manner that reflects both the nature of the giver and the gift. This way of life is dedicated to self-sacrifice in service to others. We cannot receive the gift of life adequately—nor can we fully live in an authentically human way—without making our own lives a gift to others: a gift of ourselves to our spouse and then, in turn, to our children. This community of persons in which the unconditional gift of self is taken up as a way of life is the primary way in which the family shines as a domestic church. John Paul II believed that "Through the family passes the primary current of the civilization of love."[33]

The family is the first and greatest bulwark against the encroachment of lifelessness and materialism on contemporary culture. This is because, in the first place, the family is the setting in which new life is brought into the world and nurtured to the point where it can survive independently. Just as important, the family is the vehicle for transmitting to the rising generation the values that will shape it and guide it into the future. If the truths of human existence and destiny are to be imparted to our children, it will happen primarily in this nexus. For this reason it is no exaggeration to say that the ultimate fate of the human race lies in the family. And the ultimate fate of the family lies in the integrity of the intimate life of husband and wife.

Since the Second Vatican Council, the Catholic Church has increasingly focused on the family as a context for living the Christian life. Today, it is increasingly common to speak of the family as the "domestic church." This is not merely rhetorical. The ideal of the family as the domestic church goes back to the Old Testament. It was stated most simply and eloquently, perhaps, by Joshua: "As for me and my house, we will serve the LORD."[34] It was developed in the New Testament: "Husbands, love your wives, as Christ loved the church and gave himself up for her."[35] And it has been treated many times since then by the

great thinkers of Christianity. The Church Father St. John Chrysostom (A.D. 347–407), for example, wrote, "Make of your home a
church, because you are accountable for the salvation of your children and your servants."[36]

Developing further this ancient idea of the Christian family as
a domestic church, John Paul II often remarked that he viewed
the Christian family as the primary point of encounter between
the church and culture. Consequently, he encouraged a deep pastoral reflection on the role of the Christian family that is only in
its beginnings. The challenge to theologians and pastors is clearly
presented in the following statement by John Paul II:

> The family itself is the great mystery of God. As the "do-
> mestic church," it is the bride of Christ. The Universal Church,
> and every Particular Church in her, is most immediately re-
> vealed as the bride of Christ in the "domestic church" and in
> its experience of love: conjugal love, paternal love and ma-
> ternal love, fraternal love, the love of a community of per-
> sons and of generations.

John Paul II stressed that "in the future, evangelization will
depend largely on the domestic Church."[37] How? Not many families
are likely to take an active role in evangelizing as such. And although
the family is the means by which the Christian faith is handed down
from generation to generation, even this fact does not exhaust the
meaning of John Paul II's assertion. Rather he is saying that the
family is—and will be—the chief witness to the active power of the
love of God in the world. "The essence and role of the family are in
the final analysis specified by love. Hence the family has the mission
to guard, reveal, and communicate love, and this is a living reflection
and a real sharing in God's love for humanity and the love of Christ
the Lord for the Church His bride."[38]

Cardinal Scola suggests an important dimension in this consideration. He writes, "In defining the family as 'domestic church,'

Vatican Council II opened the way to a consideration of the family as a dimension of evangelization. The reality of the church as universal sacrament of salvation is present in the family and is so with a particular concreteness and clarity that are not owed simply to the fact that the family is that reality which reaches farthest into the ultimate expression of the human."[39] Yet, Scola maintains that, "it is the sacramentality of marriage that makes the family objectively a 'domestic church,' and thus a dimension of evangelization." Because of the sacramental character of marriage, the Christian family "is the most common, universal, and basic expression of the manner in which Christ is joined to the church" and because of that "the family carries within itself the deep meaning that the church has for the world: the enduring presence of Christ."[40]

When we understand the family as "domestic church" in light of the sacramental nature of marriage, we are able to see that in their commitment to the family, Christian husbands and wives carry out both their vocation as spouses and their vocation as laymen and laywomen to renew and evangelize society. John Paul II proposed a profound renewal of the sacramental understanding of marriage and in this way has also proposed a profound renewal of Christian family life through the appreciation of the family as domestic church. In doing so, he echoed the words of Tertullian from the earliest centuries of Christianity: "How can I ever express the happiness of the marriage that is joined together by the Church, strengthened by an offering, sealed by a blessing, announced by angels and ratified by the Father? How wonderful the bond between two believers, with a single hope, a single desire, a single observance, a single service! They are both brethren and both fellow-servants; there is no separation between them in spirit or flesh; in fact they are truly two in one flesh, and where the flesh is one, one is the spirit."[41]

SUGGESTIONS FOR CONTEMPLATION AND ACTION

1. Spend some time reflecting on the family you grew up in. What were the key values that you were raised with? How do you express these values in your life today?

2. When you read or watch media news, look for instances in which life is spoken of in impersonal or mechanical terms, particularly regarding issues like abortion and stem-cell research. How are the attitudes of mass culture shaping this discussion?

3. If you have a spouse, take some time to consider how you regard her (or him). Do you genuinely regard yourself as being joined to your spouse as "one flesh"? Is there a subtle—or powerful—sense of "my" interests as opposed to "hers" or "his"? In what parts of your marriage does this tend to manifest itself? Has it made your marriage happier or less happy?

4. Make a point sometime within the next week to do something that will bring you closer to your spouse. The practice may be most powerful if you use it as an occasion to see the other person's point of view in an area where you have been in long disagreement.

5. If you have children, look at the values they are expressing in their behavior and activities and their dress. How close are these to the highest values that you hold? Are they an expression of the truths of Christianity, or of the values of secular mass culture? If it is the latter, reflect on how you may have encouraged this tendency in them, and implement some simple ways to change it. Hint: the changes will be stronger and more long lasting if they are in your own behavior rather than mere orders imposed on your children.

6

Globalization and the Gospel of Work

In 1940, in order to avoid deportation to a concentration camp in Nazi-occupied Poland, the young Karol Wojtyla began work for the Solvay chemical company. For the first year he worked at the Solvay quarry. The work consisted of breaking up limestone and shoveling it into small railway cars or carrying it in buckets upon one's shoulder. The workers were allowed one meal during their day's labor, and that was limited to fifteen minutes. In the coldest winter months Wojtyla would smear petroleum jelly on his face to keep his skin from freezing. The small earnings he received for his labor were all he and his father had to live on, since the Nazis had canceled the retired soldier's pension. After the first year, he moved to the Solvay factory, where he worked in the water purification unit. This was his life for four years.

Within a year after Wojtyla had begun work at the quarry, his father died; a year later, while working in the factory, Wojtyla decided to become a priest. As he recounted later, "after my father's death . . . I gradually became aware of my true path, I was working at a plant and devoting myself, as far as the terrors of the occupation allowed, to my taste for literature and drama. My priestly vocation took shape in the midst of all that, like an inner fact of unquestionable and absolute clarity. The following year, in the autumn, I knew that I was called."[1]

At that time, the Poles had a word to describe the industrial worker that aptly captured Wojtyla's working conditions: *robotnik*.[2] But for him, the men with whom he worked were anything but unthinking and mechanical. Writing on the fiftieth anniversary of his priestly ordination in *Gift and Mystery*, Wojtyla, then Pope John Paul II, observed that the quarry and the factory

> became my seminary.... For me, at that point in my life, the plant was a true seminary.... At the time I did not realize how important that experience would be for me. Only later, as a priest ... did I realize how important contact with the world of work had become for the Church.... Having worked with my hands, I knew quite well the meaning of physical labor. Every day I had been with people who did heavy work. I came to know their living situations, their families, their interests, their human worth, and their dignity.... I was also able to observe their deep but quiet religiosity and their great wisdom about life.[3]

Karol Wojtyla lived the Gospel of work before he ever wrote about it as pope. Even earlier in his life, there were indications that he would understand the spiritual dimension of the Gospel of work. A classmate of his recalls that the fifteen-year-old Wojtyla entered a poetry-reading competition in his school. He chose a poem by Cyprian Norwid that included this passage:

> Beauty is not to stay hidden...
> Beauty is to make you eager to work
> And work is for a man to gain his resurrection.[4]

As John Paul II, Wojtyla would address the subject of labor on a number of occasions. To best understand his teachings, as well as the church's approach to these issues as a whole, we might want to step back and look at an encyclical promulgated in 1891 by

Pope Leo XIII. Its Latin title, *Rerum Novarum*, sounds bland when translated literally: "Of New Things."[5] But "new things"—*res novae*—is a Latin idiom meaning "revolution." It was the challenge of revolution, particularly the so-called proletarian revolution that the communist parties of Europe were then promoting, that the pope was addressing. *Rerum Novarum* remains one of the greatest and most influential encyclicals of the last 150 years. It was fundamental to the approach taken by Paul VI in his encyclical on global development, *Populorum Progressio,* and it was commemorated by a number of subsequent encyclicals, most recently John Paul II's *Centesimus Annus* ("Hundredth Anniversary") in 1991. Each of these built upon the foundation set out by *Rerum Novarum*, so in a very real sense this encyclical forms the cornerstone of modern Catholic social theory.

The time of Leo XIII was marked by tense and increasingly violent rifts between owners and workers in the wake of the Industrial Revolution. Now that industrialism had overturned centuries-old relations between owners and workers that had gone back to feudal days, many people had begun to question the basic premises on which society was built: Does anyone have the right to hold private property, or should all property be owned collectively? Should the divisions between owners and workers be overthrown? What rights and responsibilities, in a Christian society, do workers and proprietors have in regard to each other?

The Christian answers to these questions were not entirely obvious. Some pointed to the Acts of the Apostles, which said that "the company of those who believed were of one heart and soul, and no one said that any of the things which he possessed was his own, but they had everything in common,"[6] as evidence that communism was true Christianity. On the other hand, the communists and anarchists who were beginning to dominate the trade-union movement were often more committed to the destruction than to the reform of the social order and were intensely hostile to Christianity and the Catholic Church.[7]

In this stormy context, Leo XIII took the bold step of reaching out to the workers. Although personally reserved and aristocratic (and averse to giving audiences), he received a number of pilgrimages by French workingmen in the late 1880s. As Albert de Mun, a Christian socialist leader, wrote:

> Then came our pilgrimages, and you recall the triumphant reception of the workers at the Vatican where they were greeted with princely honors and where the Pope received the men of the people in their working clothes. The crowd of workers took their place on the steps of the royal staircase, surprised at this new majesty which was taking the place of the sovereigns of old. It was an unforgettable spectacle. All those who saw it remember its splendor, but not every one can measure its depth. It was not only a great manifestation; it was the solemn meeting of the Head of the Church with the envoys of the people. It was the formation of the encyclical and the beginning of a new age.[8]

Rerum Novarum, inspired in part by these audiences, struck a remarkably moderate and balanced note in an age that (like ours in some respects) was becoming more and more polarized between rich and poor. At a casual glance, this document may look dated. After all, communism has been abandoned, officially or in practice, by nearly all the nations that adopted it. But *Rerum Novarum* remains as relevant as ever, even in an age when capitalism has been proclaimed triumphant as the most viable and productive of all economic systems. This encyclical is such a landmark in Catholic social thought that it is worth examining in some depth.

Rerum Novarum is in some ways Catholicism's answer to Karl Marx, so it may surprise some people that in certain respects the encyclical echoes Marx's criticisms of capitalist society. Consider this passage from *The Communist Manifesto*, published in 1848:

The bourgeoisie, wherever it has got the upper hand, has put an end to all feudal, patriarchal, idyllic relations. It has pitilessly torn asunder the motley feudal ties that bound man to his "natural superiors," and has left no other nexus between people than naked self-interest, than callous "cash payment." It has drowned out the most heavenly ecstasies of religious fervor, of chivalrous enthusiasm, of philistine sentimentalism, in the icy water of egotistical calculation.[9]

Compare Leo XIII's words:

We clearly see, and on this there is general agreement, that some opportune remedy must be found quickly for the misery and wretchedness pressing so unjustly on the majority of the working class: for the ancient workingmen's guilds were abolished in the last century, and no other protective organization took their place. Public institutions and the laws set aside the ancient religion. Hence, by degrees it has come to pass that working men have been surrendered, isolated and helpless, to the hardheartedness of employers and the greed of unchecked competition.[10]

Both of these passages portrayed the problem in a very similar light, but Leo's solution was very different from Marx's. Unlike Marx, Leo did not want to abolish private property: "Every man has by nature the right to possess property as his own," he wrote.[11] Since "all human subsistence is derived either from labor on one's own land, or from some toil, some calling, which is paid for either in the produce of the land itself, or in that which is exchanged for what the land brings forth,"[12] it is only reasonable that people should have the right to own the land in which they have invested time and labor. In addition, Leo, echoing what we have already seen is a deeply rooted emphasis on the family in the Catholic tradition, insisted that it is private property that enables a father to provide for his children. Hence he strenuously opposed the Marxists' proposed abolition of private property.

Leo went on to condemn another Marxist doctrine: that everyone should be reduced—forcibly if necessary—to a state of absolute equality. "It is impossible to reduce civil society to one dead level," Leo wrote. "People differ in capacity, skill, health, strength; and unequal fortune is a necessary result of unequal condition."[13]

To a degree, then, Leo would seem to have been an upholder of the status quo. But he was not. The age in which Leo was writing was a time when virtually all the economic power in the workplace lay in the hands of the owners of the mills and factories in which the workers toiled. Laws ensuring safe working conditions, a minimum wage, or the right to collective bargaining did not exist. In this era, Leo laid out moral responsibilities for the owners—responsibilities that many of them felt they did not have:

> The employer must never tax his work people beyond their strength, or employ them in work unsuited to their sex and age. His great and principal duty is to give every one what is just. . . . To exercise pressure upon the indigent and the destitute for the sake of gain, and to gather one's profit out of the need of another, is condemned by all laws, human and divine. To defraud any one of wages that are his due is a great crime which cries to the avenging anger of Heaven. . . . Lastly, the rich must religiously refrain from cutting down the workmen's earnings, whether by force, by fraud, or by usurious dealing; and with all the greater reason because the laboring man is, as a rule, weak and unprotected, and because his slender means should in proportion to their scantiness be accounted sacred. Were these precepts carefully obeyed and followed . . . , would they not be sufficient of themselves to keep under all strife and all its causes?[14]

These were all astonishingly courageous statements to make in the social climate of 1891, but the last sentence may contain the greatest insight in *Rerum Novarum*. Communism was struggling to overthrow the social structure in the hope that a level playing field would ensure economic justice. In fact it did not; "unequal fortune" and "unequal condition" would reappear almost immediately in the societies that, in attempting the communist experiment, exterminated or exiled their propertied classes. This leads to a striking but often overlooked conclusion: social engineering, even if well intended, cannot in itself create a just society. A just society must arise out of the hearts and minds of those who live in it. If the precepts that Leo proposed—which are, after all, specific applications of the natural law—were voluntarily obeyed by all people, the need for complicated laws and governments would be greatly reduced. This truth, being universal, has been stated many times, for example, in the ancient Chinese classic known as the *Tao Te Ching*:

> When Tao is lost, there is goodness.
> When goodness is lost, there is kindness.
> When kindness is lost, there is justice.
> When justice is lost, there is ritual.
> Now ritual is the husk of faith and loyalty, the beginning of confusion.[15]

Tao is a difficult word to translate. It is sometimes rendered as the "way," "truth," or even "meaning." In this instance we might take the bold step of translating it as *love*. As Leo wrote, "if Christian precepts prevail, the respective classes will not only be united in the bonds of friendship, but also in those of brotherly love."[16] When love is lost, it must be replaced by rules. But these will never be entirely adequate. No rules can be made that will apply perfectly to all situations, and in any case people can be remarkably cunning in complying with the letter of the law while undermining its spirit. Christ's rebukes of the scribes and Pharisees of his day bring home this truth vividly. The wisest solution is a dual one: to remember that love is the paramount consideration in our dealings with others ("Love and do what thou wilt," said St. Augustine),[17] while setting structures of justice and equity in place that will enable this love to flourish in society.

To take one example, although Leo wrote, "the Church . . . tries to bind class to class in friendliness and good feeling," he was well aware that, given human nature, this effort might not be enough in itself. Consequently—and this was a radical step in his day—he affirmed the rights of workingmen to bargain collectively, that is, to unionize.[18] Furthermore, he admonished the civil authorities to care for the working classes in writing and administering the laws: "The richer class have many ways of shielding themselves, and stand less in need of help from the State; whereas the mass of the poor have no resources of their own to fall back upon, and must chiefly depend upon the assistance of the State."[19] Among the social-welfare measures he advocated are limits to the working day: "Daily labor . . . should be so regulated as not to be protracted over longer hours than strength admits."[20]

In short, Leo XIII advocated the spirit of "friendliness and good feeling" among the classes of society, but he also set out conditions by which this good feeling can be attained. His recommendations proved to be remarkably wise and foresighted. Forty years later, Pope Pius XI could write that "the statesmen of the leading nations . . . [gave] sanction to many points that so remarkably coincide with Leo's principles and instructions as to seem consciously taken therefrom."[21]

Where do we stand today in regard to the issues Leo addressed? What working conditions did John Paul II face and does Benedict have to face now? On one hand, standards of living, safety, comfort, and health care are far beyond what anyone in the late nineteenth century would have dreamed possible. On the other hand, there are alarming signs that some social conditions are not improving or even holding steady. One example is the amount of hours Americans are working. The Fair Labor Standards Act of 1938 set a forty-hour work week, but today more than 40 percent of U.S. workers are working more than fifty hours per week.

Part of the reason for this trend, according to Joe Robinson, author of *Work to Live*, is the burgeoning of salaried positions. Originally, salaried positions—jobs for which the individual is paid a flat amount of money regardless of the number of hours worked—were meant to be for top and middle management. In 1940 managers and salaried professionals accounted for less than 9 percent of the work force.[22] Today, however, more than 40 percent of all U.S. workers are salaried. Some companies perceive a vested interest in getting as many hours as possible out of a given employee. In such situations, are companies honoring the principle that daily labor should not be "protracted over longer hours than strength admits"?

Very often such forms of exploitation are not even cost-effective. Robinson observes, "Chronic 11- and 12-hour days result in lousy productivity, expensive mistakes, burnout, triple the risk of heart attack and quadruple the risk of diabetes—and families without a quorum for dinner. Two-thirds of people who work more than 40 hours a week report being highly stressed. Job stress costs American business more than $300 billion a year."[23]

Robinson's aside about "families without a quorum for dinner" should not be glossed over. Today we lament the decline of the family, the increasing isolation and alienation of family members from one another, and the social problems that result. Does this decline have anything to do with the encroachment of the workday into times that were formerly devoted to family life? When parents come home after a twelve-hour day too exhausted to do more than barely acknowledge their children's existence, or when they relegate their children's upbringing to the electronic nanny known as television, quality of life begins to decline. Sociologist Arlie Russell Hochschild writes, "Over the last two decades, American workers have increasingly divided into a majority who work too many hours and a minority with no work at all. . . . For [the long-hours majority], a speeding up at the office and factory has marginalized life at home, so that the very term 'work-family balance' seems to many a bland slogan with little bearing on real life."[24]

These realities have bearing not only on how parents interact with children but on how they feel toward them. Hochschild asked one executive whether he wished he had spent more time with his three daughters when they were growing up. This is how she describes his response:

> "Put it this way, I'm pleased with how they turned out." The father loved his daughters, but he loved them as results. Or rather, his feeling was "I want my wife to enjoy the process of raising them. I'll enjoy that vicariously. What I will enjoy directly is the result, the young adults."[25]

One of the key features of the work ethic as commonly understood is deferred gratification, the capacity to put off enjoying the fruits of one's labor until the labor is done. But we can ask whether deferring the enjoyment of one's children is healthy or productive for oneself, or for one's children.

Another aspect of this trend is the increasing secularization of Sunday. A generation ago, very few businesses were open on Sunday; many states forbade them by law from doing so. Today there are few retail stores that are not open on Sunday, and more and more businesses of other kinds are also operating on the concept of a seven-day week. (How often do we hear "24–7" invoked as a kind of rallying call to optimum performance?) It's tempting to dwell on the remarkable convenience this provides for us—but it is well to remember that the convenience is for us *as consumers*.

We have more time and leisure for shopping and spending, but this may be time and leisure that are being subtracted from more important areas of life.

To go back to *Rerum Novarum*, Leo speaks of "the obligation of the cessation from work and labor on Sundays and certain holy days." He explains: "Rest (combined with religious observances) disposes man to forget for a while the business of his everyday life, to turn his thoughts to things heavenly, and to the worship which he so strictly owes to the eternal Godhead. It is this, above all, which is the reason and motive of Sunday rest."[26] It's worth asking whether a return to a stricter and more general Sunday observance would help remedy many of the problems of stress, deterioration of family life, and alienation that are so widely lamented today.

Many read *Rerum Novarum* as a sort of social and economic platform, much like the policy platforms of political parties, and in some respects the encyclical can be understood that way. We can list the principles articulated by Leo, such as the right to private property, the right of inheritance, the dignity of workers, their right to organize in unions, their right to a just wage and a family wage, the regulation of child labor, the right to equitable and fair taxes, the right to form associations for mutual aid, and so forth. Similarly, because of its defense of the dignity and rights of workers, *Rerum Novarum* has been described as the Magna Carta of the church's social doctrine. Nonetheless, *Rerum Novarum* and the other social encyclicals are far more than policy pronouncements. As John Paul II emphasizes in his encyclicals *Laborem Exercens* (*On Human Work*), written in 1981, and *Centesimus Annus*, we need to focus on the central foundation from which such policies arise. John Paul II writes in *Centesimus Annus*, "From this point forward it will be necessary to keep in mind that the main thread and, in a certain sense, the guiding principle of Pope Leo's encyclical, and of all of the Church's social doctrine, is a *correct view of the human person* and of his unique value."[27]

To see what John Paul II means, we can turn to *Laborem Exer-cens*. Significantly, this document begins its discussion of "work and man" with Genesis, particularly the verse in which God commands the primordial man, "Be fruitful and multiply, and fill the earth and subdue it; and have dominion over the fish of the sea and over the birds of the air and over every living thing that moves upon the earth."[28] John Paul II comments, "Man has to subdue the earth and dominate it, because as the 'image of God' he is a person, that is to say, a subjective being capable of acting in a planned and rational way, capable of deciding about himself and with a tendency to self-realization." That is to say, human participation supplies an element in nature that would be otherwise lacking: reason and conscious purpose. Because of this, the pope continues, "human work has an ethical value of its own."[29] Of course, this reason and purpose must not be exploitative. Rather, as many Christian commentators have interpreted it, the command to "have dominion over" nature refers to compassionate stewardship, or, using the language of Genesis again, to "till" and "keep" the garden.[30]

The program of Genesis is brought to fulfillment in Christ, who "devoted most of the years of his life on earth to *manual work* at the carpenter's bench. This circumstance constitutes in itself the most eloquent 'Gospel of work,' showing that the basis for determining the value of human work is not primarily the kind of work being done, but the fact that the one who is doing it is a person." From this it follows that "the sources of the dignity of work are to be sought primarily in the subjective dimension, not in the objective one."[31]

As John Paul II notes, this view is radically different from that of the ancient pagan world, in which manual labor was thought to be unfit for free men and worthy only for slaves. This is not simply an aesthetic point; it is fundamentally anthropological. For Christianity, the meaning of human life is to be found in work. In the words of the poem recited by the young Karol

Wojtyla, "work is for a man to gain his resurrection." The dignity of work constitutes one of the inalienable rights of the human person.

John Paul II was highly critical of systems that stripped both people and labor of their essential dignity. Certainly this included Marxism. Historians have attributed the collapse of the communist bloc in the 1980s and 1990s in part to John Paul II's moral influence, emphasizing his concentration on "worker solidarity" and the repeated use of the term "solidarity" and its significant influence on events in Poland during the 1980s. Polish workers picked up the theme of solidarity, using it as the name for the movement that helped bring about the end of communism in that country. John Paul II was the victim of an assassination attempt on May 13, 1981, for which the Italian government has recently placed responsibility on the Soviet Union. Interestingly the attack occurred two days before the scheduled release of *Laborem Exercens*.

While communism is an extreme case of the tendency to alienate humanity from the dignity of its own labor (ironically the same fault that Marx decried in capitalism), such attitudes can be found in any system that views human life solely in economic terms. Some in the West criticized *Laborem Exercens* for asserting that "'rigid' capitalism must undergo continual revision in order to be reformed."[32] But capitalism past and present has been guilty of these shortcomings. More important, capitalism past and present has shown itself capable of reform.

The philosopher Alain de Botton observes:

> To maximise output, every organisation will strive to obtain its necessary raw materials, labour and machinery at the lowest possible cost and combine them to turn out a product that it will then attempt to sell at the highest possible price. From a purely economic perspective, there is no distinction to be made among any of the elements on the input side of the equation. . . .

And yet, troublingly, there is one difference between "labour" and other commodities, a difference that conventional economics does not have a means of representing or giving weight to but that is nevertheless unavoidably present in the world: that labour feels pain.[33]

Any system that ignores this truth, that fails to regard the human being as a living subject, could be called many things, but it could not be called Christian. John Paul II writes of consumer society: "Insofar as it denies an autonomous existence and value to morality, law, culture, and religion, it agrees with Marxism, in the sense that it totally reduces man to the sphere of economics and the satisfaction of material needs.[34]

A hardheaded businessman may say that it is all very well to have these sentiments, but the ultimate reality is the bottom line, and the bottom line does not consider human feelings. But, one may reply, whom does the bottom line serve? Is it a god to be worshiped in its own right? John Paul II writes:

Profitability is not the only indicator of a firm's condition. It is possible for the financial accounts to be in order, and yet for the people—who make up the firm's most valuable asset—to be humiliated and their dignity offended. Besides being morally inadmissible, this will eventually have negative repercussions on the firm's economic efficiency. In fact, the purpose of a business firm is not simply to make a profit, but is to be found in its very existence as a community of persons who in various ways are endeavouring to satisfy their basic needs, and who form a particular group at the service of the whole of society. Profit is a regulator of the life of a business, but it is not the only one; other human and moral factors must also be considered which, in the long term, are at least equally important for the life of a business.[35]

There is a delicate balance to be struck here. A business is not a charity. It cannot be expected to run deficits indefinitely simply for the sake of good will. On the other hand, many business-people are tempted to say—in the privacy of their hearts, if not in public—that "human and moral factors" may need to be considered, but later, when current problems are solved, when the market is not so cutthroat, when business is on a more stable footing—that is, in a future that is indefinitely postponed.

Unquestionably the nineteenth-century industrialists against whose greed Leo XIII inveighed would have said much the same thing. When business is viewed in terms of mere short-term profitability, humaneness and morality may never look advantageous. Some managers even regard these things almost as a dereliction of duty. They believe that they are responsible to the shareholders alone—a belief that takes its toll on workers every day. In Studs Terkel's classic oral history *Working*, a spot-welder tells of his experience on an auto assembly line:

One night a guy hit his head on a welding gun. He went to his knees. He was bleeding like a pig, blood was oozing out. So I stopped the line for a second and ran over to help him. The foreman turned the line on again, he almost stepped on the guy. That's the first thing they always do. They didn't even call an ambulance. The guy walked to the medic department—that's about half a mile—he had about five stitches in his head.

The foreman didn't say anything. He just turned the line on. You're nothing to any of them. That's why I hate the place.[36]

The great social encyclicals have told us that this view, in which workers are "nothing to any of them," is immoral and un-Christian. But our experience of industrialization within Western nations during the nineteenth and twentieth centuries should make us better appreciate the experiences of the equally dramatic course of economic development globally, especially the impact on poor, developing countries. In this regard, there is an important lesson to be learned from India's great independence leader, Mohandas Gandhi. We know that Gandhi's moral philosophy of nonviolent change greatly influenced leaders such as Martin Luther King Jr. and Nelson Mandela. But it has been suggested that one of Gandhi's greatest insights was that he perceived "a new type of ethics was emerging in the world"—ethics grounded in *empathy*.[37] In other words, ethical decision making should be connected to the ability to place one's self in the circumstances of the other person. Language, customs, religion, geography, and family life differ widely around the globe. But there is common ground in the experience of industrialization. Those of us living in developed nations need to appreciate that reality if we are to pursue greater economic interdependence while reducing the number of people in developing nations who will say of globalization, "I hate this place."

For more than a century, the Catholic Church has significantly changed the course of economic development in the West. Toward the end of the nineteenth century, *Rerum Novarum* contributed in a remarkable way to the reform—we might even go so far as to say "humanization"—of capitalism. This was followed toward the end of the twentieth century by *Laborem Exercens* and its substantial repudiation of Marxist economic theory and its development of a Christ-centered "Gospel of work." There is no reason now why Catholics cannot build upon this foundation to dramatically influence the future course of globalization.

In *Populorum Progressio,* Paul VI suggested precisely this when he stated that the principles articulated by Leo XIII in *Rerum Novarum* not only still have application today within national economies, but they should be applied to economic relations *between* nations concluding that "Free trade can be called just only when it conforms to the demands of social justice."[38]

John Paul II recognized in *Centesimus Annus* that globalization "can create unusual opportunities for greater prosperity."[39] Today the statement would seem remarkable for its understatement. Nobel Prize winner Gary S. Becker observes that "As a result of the movement toward an integrated world economy, global income grew at its fastest rate in recorded history. World population more than doubled from 1950 to the end of the twentieth century. Yet real per capita income grew, on average, by about 2 percent a year around the world." More important, according to Becker, is the fact that "the per capita gross domestic product of poorer nations grew about as fast as that of richer nations, whereas populations in the less developed world grew much more rapidly."[40]

We might consider the situation from the standpoint of the number of persons on the planet living in dire poverty—living on less than two dollars per day. As we ended the twentieth century, nearly 1 billion persons lived on less than two dollars per day, and of those, approximately 300 million lived on less than one dollar. Yet, only twenty-five years earlier, those numbers were respectively 1.5 billion and 700 million. Again, it is important to remember that this decline in poverty occurred during a time when global population increased from 4 billion to 6 billion.[41] According to Ernesto Zedillo, director of the Yale Center for the Study of Globalization and former president of Mexico, "The market economy's capacity to fulfill human needs is being enhanced to an unprecedented extent by international trade and investment."[42]

Of course, such new opportunities to increase living standards are enormously attractive throughout the developing world. Groups that have had no experience of bettering their lives or those of their children suddenly see prospects of a better life. But this progress often comes at a cost. Too often the way in which the market economy fulfills human needs comes at the cost of disrupting, displacing, and even discarding society's higher values. Paul VI warned of this danger when he wrote in 1968:

> Every country, rich or poor, has a cultural tradition handed down from past generations. This tradition includes institutions required by life in the world, and higher manifestations—artistic, intellectual and religious—of the life of the spirit. When the latter embody truly human values, it would be a great mistake to sacrifice them for the sake of the former. Any group of people who would consent to let this happen, would be giving up the better portion of their heritage; in order to live, they would be giving up their reason for living. Christ's question is directed to nations also: "What does it profit a man, if he gain the whole world but suffer the loss of his own soul?"[43]

That is a price we have refused to pay in the West, and we should not demand of others around the world such a price for economic development. To the contrary, true development can only proceed in the long term when it is based upon spiritual and moral values. Paul VI insisted that we must work for an economic and social "transition from less than human conditions to truly human ones."[44] Catholics especially should not permit the discussion of globalization to continue in terms of a "false choice" between material progress and moral values. Benjamin Friedman suggests that a better way of looking at the problem is to begin with the recognition that economic growth (when understood as a rising standard of living for a majority of a nation's people) "more often than not fosters greater opportunity, tolerance of diversity, social mobility, commitment to fairness, and dedication to democracy."[45] Importantly, Friedman also argues that the contrary may also be generally true: "Experience clearly indicates that the absence of democratic freedoms impedes economic growth, and that the resulting stagnation in turn makes a society even more intolerant and undemocratic."[46] If this is true, then economic development, especially in the long term, depends upon the preservation of certain moral values entirely consistent with Catholic social teaching. And if this is true, then Catholics can and should endeavor to help developing nations achieve sustained economic growth.

One of the most formidable obstacles to that growth is the deeply rooted corruption in both politics and business throughout much of the developing world. Catholics can make an enormous contribution to sustained economic development by establishing greater respect for the rule of law. Former chief justice of the Philippines Hilario Davide, a friend and brother Knight of Columbus whom I got to know during a 2005 trip to Manila, is an extraordinary example of just what can be done in this regard. As a young assemblyman, Davide rallied the public against the martial law imposed by President Ferdinand Marcos. Then under the new government of Corazon Aquino, he served as a member of the Constitutional Commission helping to restore confidence in the national legislature, and later as chairman of the Commission on Elections, he helped to assure free and fair national elections. Finally, he served for more than a decade on his country's Supreme Court. Few individuals have played as decisive a role in promoting the rule of law in his country as has Hilario Davide, and he has done so with a decidedly Catholic attitude. "Administering justice," he once said, "is a sacramental task."

An end to corruption is essential to growth in Africa and Latin America. Endemic corruption in those regions is one of the foremost reasons for differences in the achievement in living standards between Asia and both Africa and Latin America. For example, in the 1950s living standards in Africa were actually 25 percent *higher* than in Asia, yet by 1975 the situation was precisely reversed: Asians enjoyed a standard of living 25 percent greater than Africans'. Today, nearly one African in two lives on less than two dollars a day—approximately one-half of all the people in the world who do so.[47] It is difficult to see a solution to the situation of poverty in the African subcontinent without a solution to the crushing burden of its foreign debt. Yet, it is equally difficult to see the possibility of wide-scale debt forgiveness while the levels of corruption in Africa remain at such extraordinary levels.

One of Paul VIs greatest legacies in the area of social and economic development is his insistence that "It is not just certain individuals but all men who are called to further the development of human society as a whole."[48]

The pope was convinced that the church of the Good Samaritan was calling each of her members to take up this great responsibility, one we should not view in a narrow fashion. One of the aspects of globalization that has created great concern is the degree to which governments have relinquished to corporations unprecedented levels of economic power and decision making. Too often the result has been that shareholder accountability has replaced accountability to the public through democratic institutions. Yet this could provide an avenue for great influence among Catholics in the corporate world to affect the course of globalization. Corporations possess resources, flexibility, and adeptness far exceeding those of many governmental agencies. They can be used to steer economic development consistent with certain moral values.

David Bornstein, author of *How to Change the World*, suggests the emergence of a new global citizen sector that is leading patterns of social and economic change throughout the developing world.[49] He describes the leaders of this citizen sector as "social entrepreneurs"—men and women who in addition to applying management skills to solve social problems do so with a new idea that has transformative power to create significant change throughout society. These people also possess a steel-like determination that enables them to overcome obstacles and see their projects through to successful conclusions even when it may take many years or decades. Bornstein acknowledges that what he describes as "social entrepreneurs" have existed throughout history—even citing St. Francis of Assisi as one example and William Lloyd Garrison (abolition of slavery), Susan B. Anthony (women's rights), and Florence Nightingale (nursing) as others. (I would include Father Michael J. McGivney, founder of the Knights of Columbus, for his contribution to Catholic fraternalism and affordable life insurance for Catholic working men whose particular legacy in the business side of the order is discussed in the next Chapter). But what is new today, Bornstein observes, is the unprecedented increase in the number of social entrepreneurs and their ability to change social conditions in the developing world.

Sargent and Eunice Shriver, by what they have accomplished through the Special Olympics to change how society regards people with intellectual disabilities, provide sterling examples of how Catholics can change a society for the better as true social entrepreneurs. Knights of Columbus have been active as volunteers for Special Olympics since the first games in Chicago in 1968, and so it was fitting that after the terrorist attacks of September 11 and the immediate effect on the airline industry, the Knights of Columbus provided one million dollars to ensure that Special Olympic athletes from throughout North America could travel to the first international games held in Dublin, Ireland, in 2003. It was a tremendous feeling to be with the American athletes on opening day and to walk out onto the field with them during the opening ceremonies. Special Olympics is indeed changing the world through the power of an idea and through the strength and determination of thousands of devoted athletes and their families. What social entrepreneurs like the Shrivers teach us is that the real power of their idea is that it empowers millions of people to act in ways that change society for the better.

Speaking in Brazil at the opening session of the Fifth General Conference of the Bishops of Latin America and the Caribbean in 2007, Pope Benedict addressed the issue of globalization. While recognizing that globalization "benefits the great family of humanity, and is a sign of its profound aspiration towards unity," he cautioned that globalization "brings with it the risk of vast monopolies and of treating profit as the supreme value." He concluded by insisting that "globalization too must be led by ethics, placing everything at the service of the human person, created in the image and likeness of God."[50]

Undoubtedly, globalization will continue. The potential benefits, especially for the world's poor, are simply too great to ignore. But to what extent will that potential be realized? Undoubtedly, too, the future of globalization will be guided by some ethical criteria. What remains to be seen is whether Catholics and especially those in business and government will choose to adopt as that ethical criteria of "serving the human person, created in the image and likeness of God." Our answer to that question will make all the difference.

Suggestions for Contemplation and Action

1. Spend some time considering the role of work in your life. How do feel about your work? Is it simply a job you do to make money? Are you contributing to a larger good?

2. Think of one way this week in which you can take some small task that is part of your job and do it better: for example, being friendlier to clients or turning in something on time that you normally do late. It would be better if this is a part of your job that you find unpleasant or disagreeable.

3. Examine your work life, and try to remember an occasion when you regarded a co-worker as less than human: as an irritation to be gotten rid of, as a disobedient servant, or

as a tyrannical master. If you were to go back to that situation, how could you treat that person as a subject rather than an object?

4. Having considered the previous question, be particularly alert for times in your work life when you may be tempted to ignore or dismiss the humanity of another. Catch yourself in the middle of the process, if possible, and find another way of behaving.

5. Think of some occasion in the recent past when you felt obliged to say no to someone in your family for the sake of work—missing a child's play or sporting event, for example, or refusing the chance to spend some extra time with your spouse. Next time, can you find the opportunity to do the opposite: to say no to work for the sake of your family? You may be tempted to jump to the conclusion that you simply can't. If so, reconsider and see if you can find another answer.

7

Ethics in the Marketplace

In his book *The Art of the Impossible: Politics as Morality in Practice*, Vaclav Havel, the playwright and former president of the Czech Republic, reviewing the terrible economic and social conditions left by over fifty years of communist rule in his country, observed:

> The worst thing is that we lived in a contaminated moral environment. We fell morally ill because we got used to saying something different from what we thought. We learned not to believe in anything, to ignore each other, to care only for ourselves. Concepts such as love, friendship, compassion, humility, and forgiveness lost their depth and dimensions. . . .
>
> The previous regime . . . reduced man to a force of production and nature to a tool of production. . . . It reduced gifted and talented people to nuts and bolts of some monstrously huge, noisy and stinking machine, whose real meaning is not clear to anyone.
>
> When I talk about contaminated moral atmosphere, I am not just talking about the [communist officials]. I am talking about all of us. We had all become used to the totalitarian system and accepted it as an unalterable fact of life, and thus we helped to perpetuate it. . . . None of us are just its victims: we are all also its co-creators.[1]

Although it would hardly be fair to claim there is a moral equivalence between communism and our free-enterprise system, Havel's description does resemble the moral atmosphere in some of today's corporate offices. One of the most disturbing films of recent years is the 2003 documentary *The Corporation*. Taking its cue from the fact that the corporation is legally a person under U.S. law, the film diagnoses this "person" as if it were a human being. Using standard psychiatric diagnostic criteria, the film-makers conclude: "The operational principles of the corporation give it a highly anti-social 'personality': It is self-interested, inherently amoral, callous and deceitful; it breaches social and legal standards to get its way; it does not suffer from guilt, yet it can mimic the human qualities of empathy, caring and altruism."[2]

Clearly the film's blanket condemnation of corporations is too extreme. Many, probably most, companies are good "corporate citizens." Even so, there is a mentality in the business world that has resulted in "the monstrously huge, noisy and stinking machines" known as Enron, Global Crossing, and WorldCom. When the Enron scandal broke several years ago, many were shocked to learn of the flagrancy of the fraud. In a notorious taped conversation, one Enron employee complains to another, "They're [expletive] taking all the money back from you guys? . . . All the money you guys stole from those poor grandmothers in California?" "Yeah, grandma Millie, man," the other employee cynically replies.[3]

While these are the most visible cases, ethical lapses are common and widespread as the recent crisis resulting from sub-prime mortgage investment practices makes clear. It is not always a matter of breaking the law. People can be remarkably skillful at staying within the letter of the law while violating its intent. In his book *The New Economy*, Roger Alcaly, a well-known writer on finance and economics, notes that in the heady days of the late 1990s, "many companies took advantage of opportunities to deceive investors that were available under standard accounting rules [*sic*] . . . using them to create financial results that were misleading but did not violate specific regulations."[4]

Even duty to the shareholders—that *summum bonum* of management—is not an absolute. William W. George, professor of management practice at the Harvard Business School and a director of several corporations including ExxonMobil and Goldman Sachs, has criticized the "shareholder-value mantra," driven by pressure from Wall Street, that limits the thinking of many managers.[5] Duty to shareholders is *one* responsibility of a company and its managers, but it is far from the *only* responsibility.

In short, there is a place for ethical decision making in business, and that place is everywhere. In many respects this is little more than a matter of ordinary honesty and decency. Peter F. Drucker, one of the twentieth century's most admired theorists of management, writes, somewhat dismissively, about business ethics:

> Businessmen, we are told solemnly, should not cheat, steal, lie, bribe, or take bribes. But nor should anyone else. Men and women do not acquire exemption from ordinary rules of personal behavior because of their work or job. Nor, however, do they cease to be human beings when appointed vice president, city manager, or college dean. And there has always been a number of people who cheat, steal, lie, bribe, or take bribes. The problem is one of moral values and moral education, of the individual, the family, of the school. But neither is there a separate ethics of business, nor is one needed.
>
> All that is needed is to mete out stiff punishments to those—whether business executives or others—who yield to temptation.[6]

Drucker's points are obvious and somewhat simplistic. After all, "stiff punishments" are and have long been meted out, and yet scandals and crimes seem to be as prevalent in the business world as ever. Human beings who lie, cheat, and steal are deterred only partially and imperfectly by the regulators or the police. The judicial system punished the perpetrators of the Enron scandal, but the penalties were in force beforehand and clearly did not scare them away from committing their crimes. Enforcement is not an ideal solution but a last resort. Furthermore, as the last century taught us in sad and indeed horrifying ways, individual morality, as necessary as it is, may not always suffice. People may behave decently as individuals and abominably en masse. Business is a collective enterprise, and the collective dilution of guilt sometimes appears to excuse or enable actions that individuals would never dare try on their own.

Even so, people are tempted, and at times they succumb to temptation. In other situations, reasonable persons act honorably and with the best of intentions, and yet later on, those intentions may look morally questionable. I am not suggesting that moral perfection in business or anywhere else is possible. But we have to ask whether there may be another "art of the impossible"—business as morality in practice.

I believe that ethical decision making should permeate every aspect of a company's life. Ethics should provide the context for product development, marketing, investments, and employee relationships. Indeed a moral purpose can and should serve as the very reason for a company's existence.

James Collins and Jerry Porras made one of the most important contributions to this discussion with their book *Built to Last: Successful Habits of Visionary Companies*. The authors studied some of the largest and most successful companies in American history in an attempt to understand how companies that could be described as "the best of the best" succeeded decade after decade while their nearest competitors did not.

One of their most important findings was to reject the contention that "the most successful companies exist first and foremost to maximize profits." The authors found that maximizing shareholder wealth "has not been the dominant driving force or primary objective" of these companies. Making money is only one of a cluster of priorities for these companies—and not necessarily the primary one. "They seek profits, but they're equally guided by . . . core values and sense of purpose beyond just making money." Yet, paradoxically, the authors "found that the visionary companies make more money than the more purely profit-driven comparison companies."[7] When one reflects upon the various examples of what the authors describe as a company's "core ideology," one usually finds an ethical component within the company's vision—and a sense of caring that goes far beyond the bottom line.

In 1906, for example, A. P. Giannini's Bank of Italy had been in business for only two years when it was hit by the great San Francisco earthquake. Undaunted, Giannini took two million dollars in gold and securities in a horse-drawn carriage and set up business on a wharf the next day. Much of Giannini's money would go toward rebuilding the devastated city. But Giannini's genius went far further than that. He was the first in the banking industry to focus on the needs of working-class people, a group that up to that point had been ignored as not being creditworthy. He also offered a favorable lending environment for farmers and small businesspeople, and the Bank of America that he built as a result grew into one of the largest and most successful financial institutions in the world.[8]

Thus, despite the impression given by recent scandals in the business world, we should remember that not only is it possible to conduct business from a moral standpoint, but it is also possible to do so in a way that is successful. A strong ethical stance may even further a company's success. These are lessons we have learned at the Knights of Columbus.

Most people know the Knights of Columbus as a volunteer Catholic men's organization involved in charitable projects in members' local communities. But the organization is also a fraternal benefit society that sells life-insurance products to its members and through them to their families. Indeed this purpose was a central reason for the Knights' creation. The history of the Knights is an unusual and fascinating one, and it's worth examining in some detail.

The Knights of Columbus began in the nineteenth century, a time when the Industrial Revolution had created a tremendous economic boom but had also caused a tremendous amount of social dislocation. Living and working conditions in this new industrialized economy were often shockingly bad. Features of life that we now regard as necessities—health insurance, safety regulations, and disability coverage—were nonexistent. Workers often had to function in extremely hazardous conditions that were simply taken for granted. Workers in many industries ran high risks of death or disability on the job. If a man became disabled so that he was no longer able to work, he could usually expect to lose his position without any benefits. If a breadwinner died—either on the job or from any other cause—his family would very likely be left destitute.

Insurance did exist in those days, but it was expensive and chiefly covered business losses to fire, accidents, and maritime disasters. Life insurance was a luxury available only to the rich. Moreover, insurance regulation was primitive or nonexistent, and the industry was plagued by scandals and panics. For these reasons, very little insurance was available to the working classes.

As the nineteenth century progressed, a number of organizations grew up to remedy this lack. They were generically known as *benevolent associations*. Many of them were connected with the fraternal orders, of which there was a dizzying array in mid-nineteenth-century America. These orders were intended in large part to promote brotherhood and good feeling among their members, but many also offered insurance benefits. Dues-paying members were entitled to some financial compensation for themselves or their families if they were disabled or died. Some of these organizations, such as the Brotherhood of Locomotive Engineers, the Brotherhood of Railroad Trainmen, and the Sons of Vulcan (for boiler workers), were oriented toward particular trades. Others, such as the Ancient Order of Foresters and the Modern Wood-men of America, were, despite their names, not linked to any trade.[9] By the 1880s it was becoming clear to Catholic clergy and laymen alike that a benevolent association was needed that was specifically geared toward Catholics.

The decisive step was taken in 1881 by Father Michael J. McGivney, a twenty-nine-year-old parish priest in New Haven, Connecticut. McGivney was "a great favorite with the people," two of his friends would later recount in a memoir. He was especially popular "with the energetic, pushing, go-ahead young men," and he "possessed a captivating smile, and an earnestness of manner that he imparted to all whose interest and influence he sought."[10]

Like Giannini, the young priest wanted to help working-class people. Hoping to provide a new opportunity for Catholic men, McGivney called together some prominent members of his parish on October 2, 1881, to form an organization whose object, in his words, was:

To unite the men of our Faith throughout the Diocese of Hartford, that we may thereby gain strength *to aid* each other in time of sickness; to *provide* for decent burial, and to render pecuniary assistance to the families of deceased members.[11]

Interest began to grow, and the committee reconvened on February 2, 1882. By then it was clear that the group needed a name. After several were proposed, McGivney suggested "The Sons of Columbus," a name that was later changed to "Knights of Columbus." Immediately, the committee saw the brilliance of this Columbian patronage. Catholics in the nineteenth-century

United States often lived under suspicion of anti-Americanism. Many Protestants believed that Catholics were more loyal to the pope than to their country. Adopting the name of Columbus, honored as the discoverer of America, would be seen as a patriotic gesture. It was even better that Columbus was a devout Catholic. Moreover, the name had the advantage of having no association with the Irish, who in those days formed by far the largest group of ethnic Catholics in America. Although he himself was of Irish extraction, McGivney, like many Catholic leaders of his day, wanted to ensure that American Catholicism would not be seen merely as an appendage of the Irish American community. An organization invoking Columbus could appeal to the French Canadians who were then moving down to New England from Quebec and particularly to the Italian immigrants who were beginning to make their presence felt as a major ethnic group in the United States.

The issue of secrecy was a concern for the nascent Knights of Columbus, particularly since some key figures in the Catholic hierarchy of Connecticut opposed secret societies of any type, including Catholic ones. The new organization adopted a simple and ingenious solution: the proceedings and ceremonies of the Knights of Columbus would be open to priests at any time, whether or not they were members of the order. In this way, the Knights would be seen to have nothing that conflicted with Catholic teachings or morals.

The death benefits provided by the fledgling organization were, by the standards of the time, generous and affordable. There were three grades of death benefits, paying $500, $1,000, and $1,500. After the death of a member, assessments were collected from members of the three grades: $.50, $1.00, and $1.50 each respectively. If a member became sick, he was entitled to a benefit of $5 per week, about 63 percent of average wages at that time. Based on the same average, the top-level death payout was equivalent to four years' wages, which was about $200 higher than the price of an average home.[12]

In the years since then, the organization has in no way forgotten Father McGivney's original purpose. In 2006, our membership of more than 1.7 million provided more than $143 million to charity and more than sixty-four million hours of volunteer service. We also sold more than $6.5 billion of life insurance to our members. Today the Knights of Columbus has over $64 billion of insurance in force and more than $13 billion of assets under management.

The Knights of Columbus is also one of only five insurance corporations out of approximately twelve hundred in North America that have received the highest ratings from Standard and Poor's and A. M. Best as well as certification for ethical marketing practices by the Insurance Marketplace Standards Association. In its credit rating of the Knights of Columbus, Standard and Poor's has stated that its "AAA" rating was based upon the following strengths: extremely strong capital, very strong competitive position, extremely strong liquidity, and historically strong profitability. We have found that we were able to achieve that "extremely strong" capital position, that "very strong" competitive position, and that "historically strong" profitability *precisely because* we placed ethical values ahead of all of these objectives. We have achieved what Standard and Poor's described as "a distinct competitive advantage" as a result of our "loyal customer base" and our "unique rapport with clients." And we have been able to achieve such a strong relationship because we have been steadfastly committed to our motto, "Protecting Families for Generations."

That commitment is an essential core value of the Knights of Columbus as a business enterprise. It is these values and not solely the search for profits that have made our successes possible. Our core values permeate all levels of our marketing program. Our Marketing Code of Ethics is modeled after the Ten Commandments and includes statements such as "Thou shall present, honestly and accurately, all facts necessary to enable a member to make an informed decision." And our ethical principles for marketing are summed up by our Golden Rule: "In all my professional relationships, I pledge myself to the following rule of conduct: I shall, in light of all conditions surrounding those I serve, render that service which, under the same circumstances, I would apply to myself."

The Insurance Marketplace Standards Association has cited the Knights of Columbus as one of the leaders in the insurance industry for ethical sales and has identified numerous areas where we provide a model for best industry practices.

We have also initiated a mandatory third-party mediation process whereby complaints are handled without recourse to lengthy legal proceedings. Policyholders who have a complaint are represented by council in the mediation process without cost to themselves. We believe that a Catholic company ought to be able to have a system of dispute resolution that does not depend upon trial attorneys and lengthy court proceedings.

We also provide ethical criteria for the investments we make in order to reflect the moral teachings of the Catholic Church. Particular attention is paid to the product lines of companies whose debt and equity securities we consider. In this regard, we use six criteria to screen our investments. We will not invest in companies that are involved in abortion, contraception, pornography, for-profit healthcare, embryonic-stem-cell research, or human cloning. As a result, there are nearly sixty companies trading on the New York Stock Exchange and the NASDAQ in which we will not invest. We have consistently applied these ethical criteria to our investments and therefore have refused to invest in companies that many analysts insist are superior investments. Nevertheless, we have continued to achieve strong profitability year after year.

In *Laborem Exercens*, Pope John Paul II wrote, "The sources of the dignity of work are to be sought primarily in the subjective dimension, not in the objective one." The pope also said that this understanding "constitutes the fundamental and perennial heart of the Christian teaching on human work."[13] This understanding of work is essentially ethical in character because it derives first and foremost from a commitment to the dignity of the worker. It requires that all employer-employee relationships rest upon the recognition of the dignity of all the workers whose efforts combine to form the cooperative initiative that make a company's effort a success. Gifted and talented people should not be reduced to "nuts and bolts." The moment a company loses sight of the reality that its people—its employees—are its most important resource is the moment when a company begins to lose both its moral foundation and its capacity for long-term success.

Business leaders such as John Bogle, the founder of the Vanguard mutual funds, have done the country a great service in promoting a new ethical perspective for American business. The Vanguard funds are well-known for providing solid and remunerative investments with an absolute minimum of operating expenses. In his book *The Battle for the Soul of Capitalism*, Bogle insists:

> We must establish a higher set of principles. This nation's founding fathers believed in high moral standards, in a just society, and in the honorable conduct of our affairs. Those beliefs shaped the very character of our nation. If character counts, the ethical failings of today's business model, the financial manipulation of corporate America, the willingness of those of us in the field of investment management to accept practices that we know are wrong, the conformity that keeps us silent, the greed that overwhelms our reason, all erode the character that society will require of us in the years ahead. . . . Of course the successful enterprises that endure must generate profits for their owners. They will do that best when they take into account not only the interests of their stockholders but the interests of their customers, their employees, and their communities, and the interests of our society.[14]

In this effort to restore confidence and integrity to American business enterprise, Catholics have a special responsibility for leadership. I believe author Michael Novak got it right when he described "business as a calling" as one that is morally serious and that requires the practice of the virtues. His book by the same title is a good place to begin such a reflection whether one is leading a large corporation or operating his own small business.[15]

In *Centesimus Annus*, John Paul II raised the issue of the moral conditions for what he calls "an authentic 'human ecology'." All of us have an obligation to help build this moral "ecology" through the choices we make as consumers, investors, workers, and managers. Our choices are the best way we can join in this effort "to safeguard the moral conditions for an authentic 'human ecology'."[16] Moral choice is ultimately the only way that we can recognize the inherent dignity of each person and build an economy that acknowledges this dignity. Vaclav Havel was right when he reminded us that in matters of ethical deterioration, "none of us are just its victims: we are all also its co-creators." Fortunately, the opposite is also true: we all have the capacity to create a decent and responsible moral climate.

SUGGESTIONS FOR CONTEMPLATION AND ACTION

1. Think back to a time (if any) when you did something ethically questionable in the workplace. What were the circumstances? How did it happen? Was it something that you initiated, or was it the result of someone else's request or order? How did you justify it to yourself at the time? What kind of consequences did you have to face?

2. Imagine yourself in a similar moral situation that you might realistically have to face today. How would you deal with it this time? Would you be able to resist the pressure

or temptation? What did you learn from the consequences of your last ethical lapse?

3. Create an ethical "Ten Commandments" of business or professional practice for yourself.

4. Look into the stated moral principles of the company that you work for. Do you agree with them? Do they correspond to your day-to-day practice? If you are self-employed or the head of your own company, take a look at your own moral guidelines and see how well you live up to them. If you have no such guidelines, consider creating them.

5. Remember the last time you encountered an ethical breach in the workplace. How did you respond? Did you try to cover it up or paper it over? Were you a whistle-blower? Did you do your best to improve the situation without drawing attention to it? Reflect on your actions clearly and open-mindedly. Would you do the same thing again if you had the choice?

8

A People of Life and for Life

Walking through the infamous *Arbeit Macht Frei* gate leading into the Nazi death camp at Auschwitz, there is an overwhelming sense, impossible to describe, of crossing the border into a territory claimed by the culture of death. It is inconceivable that one can walk by buildings in which day after day, year after year, thousands of persons were selected for death and then killed—nearly 1.5 million men, women, and children at Auschwitz alone. To confront this reality is a staggering experience. But the attempt to express one's experience in words is inadequate to do justice to the victims. Scholars will continue to study the Holocaust, but a century from now, I fear that we will still not be able to really comprehend how such atrocities could have happened. After visiting the death camp at Buchenwald, General Dwight D. Eisenhower said, "The things I saw cannot be described in words." Perhaps in the end that is the most that can really be said.

During my first visit to Auschwitz, we found Father Maximilian Kolbe's cell in the basement of Building 11, known as the Death Block. Father Kolbe was a Polish priest who had been marked from his youth by an intense devotion to Mary Immaculate.[1] Born in 1894, he felt an early calling to the religious life. As a child, he had been somewhat mischievous, but his character changed one night after he had been scolded by his mother. "That night," he said, "I asked the Mother of God what was to become of me. Then she came to me holding two crowns, one white, the other red. She asked me if I was willing to accept either of these crowns. The white one meant that I should persevere in purity, and the red that I should become a martyr. I said that I would accept them both."

Educated at a Franciscan seminary, Kolbe was soon found to have remarkable abilities and was sent to Rome to study; there he was ordained in 1918. He returned to his native country the following year, after its independence had been restored in the aftermath of World War I. Father Kolbe believed that Poland had been liberated thanks to the Virgin Mary, and he resolved to win every heart in the nation for her. He embarked on a remarkable crusade of activity. His efforts included the establishment of a friary outside Warsaw, which he named Niepokalanow, "City of the Immaculate." The community began in 1927. By 1939, it housed over seven hundred priests, brothers, novices, and seminarians.

The outbreak of World War II in September 1939 changed Father Kolbe's mission dramatically. Within two weeks of the war's outbreak, Niepokalanow was occupied by the invading Germans. Kolbe responded by organizing a refugee center for three thousand Poles, two thousand of them Jews. In 1941, Kolbe published an issue of his journal, *The Knight of the Immaculate,* in which he fearlessly wrote:

No one in the world can change Truth. What we can do and should do is to seek truth and to serve it when we have found it. The real conflict is the inner conflict. Beyond armies of occupation and the hecatombs of extermination camps, there are two irreconcilable enemies in the depth of every soul: good and evil, sin and love. And what use are the victories on the battlefield if we ourselves are defeated in our innermost personal selves?

Soon afterward, Kolbe was arrested. In May 1941 he was sent to Auschwitz. There he suffered unimaginable torments and indignities, made worse by his tuberculosis, which had left him with only one lung. But he never lost his composure. Another priest at Auschwitz recalled: "Each time I saw Father Kolbe in the court-yard I felt within myself an extraordinary effusion of his good-ness. Although he wore the same ragged clothes as the rest of us, with the same tin can hanging from his belt, one forgot his wretched exterior and was conscious only of the charm of his in-spired countenance and of his radiant holiness."

The summer of 1941 brought Kolbe's ultimate sacrifice. In re-prisal for an escape, the Auschwitz commanders ordered that ten prisoners be interred in the notorious Death Block, where they would die agonizingly in airless underground cells without food or water. One of the men chosen cried, "Oh, my poor wife, my poor children. I shall never see them again." Kolbe stepped for-ward and offered to take the man's place. He was marched off with the two others to the Death Block.

Bruno Borgowiec, a prisoner who worked at the Death Block and so witnessed the deaths of these unfortunates, would later recollect:

> In the cell of the poor wretches there were daily loud prayers, the rosary and singing, in which prisoners from neighbouring cells also joined. When no SS men were in the Block, I went to the Bunker to talk to the men and comfort them. Fervent prayers and songs to the Holy Mother resounded in all the corridors of the Bunker. I had the impression I was in a church. Father Kolbe was leading and the prisoners responded in unison. They were often so deep in prayer that they did not even hear that inspecting SS men had descended to the Bunker; and the voices fell silent only at the loud yelling of their visitors.

These sufferings went on for two weeks, until all the other prisoners had died and only Father Kolbe was left. Eager to free

his cell for other prisoners, his captors put him to death by inject-
ing carbolic acid into his arm. "Father Kolbe, with a prayer on his
lips, himself gave his arm to the executioner," Borgowiec later
recounted.

As I stood at the site of these terrible events and prayed, I
asked myself how many times this saint (Kolbe was canonized in
1982 by his countryman, John Paul II) would have prayed the
Lord's Prayer in that room, and indeed whether the Lord's Prayer
had ever been prayed more intensely than it had been by the victims in those camps. But especially I asked myself how was it hu-
manly possible in those circumstances, without God's special
grace, to be able to say, "Forgive us our trespasses as we forgive
those who trespass against us."

Several years after my visit to Auschwitz, I had the privilege of
getting to know the late Archbishop Kazimierz Majdanski, who
became one of the first bishops in Poland to join the Knights of
Columbus. Like Father Kolbe and thousands of Polish priests and
seminarians, he, too, was sent to a Nazi death camp. But unlike so
many others, he survived the ordeal to bear eloquent testimony
to the often-overlooked suffering of Polish priests during that
time. We must never forget what occurred in Auschwitz and the
other camps. But memory is not enough. We must resolve to pre-
vent such atrocities from ever happening again. In that effort, the
elimination of anti-Semitism must continue to be a high priority
(as Kolbe's own example makes clear). This creates a special responsibility to promote respect and tolerance among all those of
religious faith, but especially for Jews. As the former Auschwitz
prisoner and Nobel Peace Prize winner Elie Wiesel has observed,
while not all victims of Nazism were Jews, all Jews were victims.

There are those who say that God was not present in such
places as Auschwitz. Others may say that if such great evil exists,
then God cannot exist. But that would grant too great a power to
human evil. As Christians, we have been promised that the gates
of hell will not prevail, no matter what may be written above

those gates. In his last book, *Memory and Identity*, Pope John Paul II discussed the mystery of evil precisely in terms of the brutal destruction of so many millions of persons in Europe during the twentieth century. He reminded us of St. Paul's words, "Do not be overcome by evil, but overcome evil with good."[2] He reminded us too that there is a "divine limit" by which "evil is radically overcome by good, hate by love, death by resurrection."[3] Evil of this magnitude cannot simply be erased. Evil must be transcended. It must be overcome. In taking on this task, we must ask ourselves: Do we have the determination to overcome a culture of death? Do we have the courage to build a truly authentic culture of life? Can we, in the words of John Paul II, truly become "a people of life and a people for life"?

Can we each day live our lives so as to avoid the temptation to regard some human beings—the poor, the handicapped, the sick, the vulnerable (whether born or unborn)—as means rather than as ends? Can we avoid the temptation of seeing some persons as having no value apart from their real or imagined use to society? In other words, can we live so as to affirm the equal dignity of every human being not only in law but in practice?

What John Paul II repeatedly described as the culture of death is inescapably a way of thinking about the value of life that rejects the essential unity of the human family in all its conditions. This way of thinking is essentially at war with the truth, because it continues to exist by rejecting, and at times even hiding, the truth regarding the nature and dignity of the human person. Because he saw this as primarily an attitude regarding respect for all human life, in his 1995 encyclical *Evangelium Vitae* (*The Gospel of Life*), he called for "a general mobilization of consciences and a united ethical effort to activate a great campaign in support of life."[4]

One of the intentions of John Paul II in writing this great encyclical was to place issues such as abortion within the broader context of the Catholic understanding of the sanctity of all human life. For this pope, it was not enough to·be against abortion. It was also necessary to work affirmatively to build conditions that would make abortion itself the wrong way of looking at such problems. And for that, it was necessary "to activate a great campaign in support of life."

The "great campaign" of which the pope wrote is something that every Catholic can join in personal and practical ways. The truth of this was brought home to me and my wife, Dorian, several years before *Evangelium Vitae* was written. We had received word that the daughter of a mutual friend had become pregnant soon after graduating high school. She did not want an abortion, but at the same time she could not face her friends and neighbors. We invited this young woman to come to Virginia and live with us. We were able to find her temporary employment, and during the time of her pregnancy she became part of our family. Both my wife and I were deeply impressed by her courage and her dedication to her child. Adoption was an option for her, but a difficult one. It was made easier by the fact that her two older brothers had been adopted by her parents as infants. She knew through firsthand experience that adoptive parents were eager to provide a loving home for the children entrusted to their care. But attending the childbirth classes and the sessions with her lawyer, it was plain to see that choosing adoption was difficult and at times very painful. In spite of it all, she allowed her first child to be adopted. Today she is married, raising her other children. I have often thought of her experience since she left our home. I continue to find her courage and dedication to her first child inspiring. I think of her every time I meet parents who have adopted a child or hear their stories. Women in these circumstances deserve a helping hand. Catholic families should be the first to offer one. I am proud that within our Knights of Columbus family so many assist crisis pregnancy centers, which make adoption a real option for these women. They are true "living stones" in building a culture of life.

During this same time, I had occasions while on trips to Rome to discuss privately with John Paul II issues regarding the legal status of abortion in the United States. I found it remarkable the concern of the pope regarding the premise that the Supreme Court used to support the legalization of abortion in its *Roe v. Wade* decision and its possible effect on democratic institutions. Supreme Court justice Harry Blackmun stated in *Roe v. Wade,* "we need not resolve the difficult question of when life begins when those trained in the respective disciplines of medicine, philosophy and theology are unable to arrive at any consensus."[5]

With this foundation in place, Justice Blackmun then went on to transform by judicial fiat what we all had understood to be a human being with potential into simply "potential human life" with an uncertain beginning. This "potential" human life was then made vulnerable to the choice of abortion. Justice Blackmun's assertion that "we need not resolve the difficult question of when life begins" has always been a rather strange assertion, but it has seemed particularly so since the birth of Louise Brown, the first so-called test-tube baby, in 1978. And equally strange is that the Supreme Court would attempt to change by its decision what we all know is true genetically: the life of each human being begins at the moment of conception.

More remarkable still was the fact that had Justice Blackmun and several of his colleagues on the Supreme Court not been so particular in selecting the case in which to consider the question of abortion, the Court's decision might have been entirely different. While *Roe v. Wade* was working its way up to the Supreme Court in 1972, another case also coming on appeal to the Supreme Court provided substantial evidence of the status of the unborn child as a human person. The case, *Byrn v. New York City Health & Hospital Corporation,*[6] presented the issue in an entirely different way than did *Roe v. Wade*.

In 1970, New York State enacted legislation that permitted abortion without restriction within the first twenty-four weeks of pregnancy. Fordham University law professor Robert Byrn obtained appointment as legal guardian for all unborn children under twenty-four weeks' gestation in New York State. He then sought to have the law declared unconstitutional as a violation of the unborn child's constitutionally protected right to life.

During the trial, Professor Byrn presented extensive expert testimony on the biological humanity of the unborn child. In fact, the trial record developed in this case was so comprehensive that the New York court concluded: "It is not effectively contradicted, if it is contradicted at all, that modern biological disciplines accept that upon conception a fetus has an independent genetic 'package' with potential to become a full-fledged human being and that it has autonomy of development and character. . . . It is human . . . and it is unquestionably alive." But then the court said, "It is not true . . . that the legal order necessarily corresponds to the natural order." The court stated that "what is a legal person is for the law . . . to say." In its view, "whether the law should accord legal personality is a policy question. . . . The point is that it is a policy determination whether legal personality should attach and not a question of biological or 'natural' correspondence."

If such language disturbs you, it also disturbed dissenting judge Adrian Burke, who wrote, "This argument was not only made by Nazi lawyers and Judges at Nuremberg, but also is advanced today by the Soviets in Eastern Europe. It was and is rejected by most western world lawyers and Judges because it conflicts with natural justice and is, in essence, irrational." In effect, Burke accused his colleagues on the New York court of accepting exactly the same argument that was rejected at the Nuremberg trials. The *Byrn* case was appealed to the Supreme Court as *Roe v. Wade* was being scheduled for rehearing. We do not know whether members of the Supreme Court studied the *Byrn* case or the issues presented by it. All we know for certain is that the court refused to fully consider the rationale for the decision in *Byrn*.

The decision in the *Byrn* case was ultimately superceded by the Supreme Court's decision in *Roe v. Wade*. But the *Byrn* case is important historically because it makes clear why *Roe v. Wade* is so problematic. First, the New York case raises the question of the adequacy of *Roe*'s trial record. If *Roe v. Wade* had included the evidence presented in the *Byrn* case, could Justice Blackmun have fairly stated that the Court was not in a position to decide when the life of a human being begins? And second, in light of the trial record in *Byrn,* it is obvious why it was so important that the case selected by Justice Blackmun and his colleagues have a certain type of trial record. A trial record that convincingly demonstrated the humanity of the unborn child would make it exceedingly difficult for a court to fashion a wide-ranging right to abortion as did the Supreme Court in *Roe v. Wade* without sounding like the New York court, that is, without sounding too much like the judges whose reasoning was condemned at Nuremberg.

It is precisely for such reasons that many Americans, Catholics and non-Catholics alike, cannot accept the Supreme Court's decision in *Roe v. Wade* as settled constitutional law. They have concluded that the entire edifice of the decision is based upon a falsehood—the denial of the biological humanity of the unborn child. They believe that some day the Supreme Court will be forced to acknowledge this fact and overturn *Roe v. Wade*. Some constitutional scholars point to the precedent of the Supreme Court's 1896 decision in *Plessy v. Ferguson* where "separate but equal" facilities for blacks and whites were found to be consistent with the Constitution. In that case the Supreme Court stated, "We consider the underlying fallacy of the plaintiff's argument to consist in the assumption that the enforced separation of the two races stamps the colored race with a badge of inferiority. If this is so, it is not by reason of anything found in the act, but solely because the colored race chooses to put that construction upon it."[7] Yet, the dissent of Justice John Marshall Harlan pointed out how the Court's reasoning presented a fictionalized account of life in segregated America: "Everyone knows," he wrote, "that the statute in question had its origin in the purpose, not so much to exclude white persons from railroad cars occupied by blacks, as to exclude colored people from coaches occupied by or assigned to white persons." Nonetheless, *Plessy v. Ferguson* remained the "settled law" of the land for fifty-eight years until it was overturned by the Supreme Court in the 1954 case of *Brown v. Board of Education*. Those who cannot support *Roe v. Wade* as "settled" law believe that one day the decision must go the way of *Plessy v. Ferguson*.

We should avoid any simplistic equation between the Nazi exterminations and today's abortions. But a society that begins to regard certain of its members as dispensable or outside the protection of the law soon may find itself sliding down a slippery slope. The Nazi killing regime of children is a case in point. It began in an extraordinary and, some might even say, *humane* way. In 1938, the father of a child born blind as well as mentally and physically handicapped wrote to Adolf Hitler, asking that his son be granted a "mercy death." Hitler agreed. Hitler had already discussed the killing of mentally ill patients at the 1935 Nazi Party Congress in Nuremberg, and the father's request provided a ready-made pretext to take action. Soon the Nazis had instituted a secret program for the mass extermination of handicapped children. Thousands were murdered in psychiatric hospitals such as Hadamar, where the administrators celebrated the ten-thousandth death with a free bottle of beer for every nurse and doctor on the staff. Of course the program was eventually extended to Jewish children and the children of other minorities.

Dr. Leo Alexander, who had studied the Nuremberg trials, sought to describe how such events could have happened. Writing in the *New England Journal of Medicine* in 1949, he said: "The beginnings at first were merely a subtle shift in emphasis in the basic attitude of the physicians. It started with the acceptance of the attitude," he continued, "that there is such a thing as life not worthy to be lived. This attitude in its early stages concerned itself merely with the severely and chronically sick. Gradually the sphere of those to be included in this category was enlarged to encompass the socially unproductive, the ideologically unwanted, the racially unwanted, and finally all non-Germans. But it is important to realize that the infinitely small wedged-in lever from which this entire trend of mind received its impetus was the attitude toward the non-rehabilitable sick."[8]

Some Catholic physicians are concerned that a similar "subtle shift in emphasis in the basic attitude of the physicians" may already have occurred in the United States as a result of *Roe v. Wade*. They cite a change in what many regard as one of the most remarkable prohibitions of abortion as well as euthanasia: the Hippocratic Oath. Originally composed in antiquity as a code of ethics for Greek doctors of the school of Hippocrates, it is used as a standard of medical ethics to this day. The original version, used in medical schools until the 1970s, requires the physician to swear: "I will neither give a deadly drug to anybody who asked for it, nor will I make a suggestion to this effect. Similarly I will not give to a woman an abortive remedy." These lines of the oath were specifically rejected by Justice Blackmun in his *Roe* opinion as now outdated. Since the Supreme Court's decision, the oath has been modified to agree with Blackmun's view: only 8 percent of these updated versions prohibit abortion, while only 14 percent prohibit euthanasia.[9] Nonetheless, it is striking that the earliest and most admired code of medical ethics specifically forbids these practices.

Hitler's programs arose out of a strong collectivist impulse— the idolization of race and blood and fatherland. That kind of impulse is not likely to arise in the increasingly diverse and multicultural United States. Ironically, though, we may reach the same predicament through exactly the opposite route: our idolization of individualism and an illusory concept of freedom. In an article in *The New Republic*, one advocate of abortion has argued that "freedom means that women must be free to choose self or to choose selfishly. . . . There is no easy way to deny the powerful argument that a woman's equality in society must give her some irreducible rights unique to her biology, including the right to take the life within her life."[10] What is most surprising here is the explicit identification of the "freedom" to perform abortion with "the right to take . . . life."

John Paul II stressed that what is at stake in the public debate regarding abortion and euthanasia is not simply a disagreement over "choices" within a pluralistic society but the very survival of democracy itself.[11] In *Evangelium Vitae*, John Paul II begins his discussion of this issue by showing a deep sensitivity toward the "tragic situations of profound suffering" that can give rise to "decisions that go against life."[12] He speaks of the "suffering, loneliness, total lack of economic prospects, depression and anxiety about the future" that can influence decisions regarding abortion, euthanasia, and suicide. Such circumstances, he adds, can even mitigate the culpability of those who make such choices, although these choices "in themselves are evil."[13]

The tragedies that lead to unfortunate decisions concerning abortion are not, however, what represents the profound threat to democracy. Such acts are called "tragedies" precisely because we know them to be wrong and we know that the person involved has submitted in desperation to circumstances she felt unable to overcome. These tragedies in themselves do not constitute a threat to democratic society, because their tragic character testifies to the objective wrong of what is done.

Instead, John Paul II contends that democratic society is imperiled by the insistence that such acts be transformed from crimes to "legitimate expressions of individual freedom . . . and protected as actual rights." This inversion of wrong actions into "right" actions constitutes "a direct threat to the entire culture of human rights." It establishes "a perverse idea of freedom" at the very heart of democracy, which "exalts the isolated individual in an absolute way, and gives no place to solidarity, to openness to others and service of them."[14]

Abortion-rights advocates claim that a true regard for pluralism and democracy requires acceptance of abortion. They argue that the social divisiveness surrounding abortion can only be resolved by their "privatization" or "deregulation." In response, John Paul II maintains that the concept of freedom implicit in abortion "rights" makes true respect for pluralism and enduring democratic structures impossible. Such an accommodation is an invitation for whole communities or classes of people to be "rejected, marginalized, uprooted and oppressed."[15] Thus freedom to perform abortion, which presents itself as essential to human freedom, instead becomes the vehicle by which the rights of many—beginning with the unborn—are threatened.

John Paul II traces the cause of this contradiction to the negation of authentic freedom. This happens when a concept of freedom is proposed that "no longer recognizes and respects its essential line with the truth"—that is, the truth about human nature. This separation of truth from freedom creates a culture in which "any reference to common values and to a truth absolutely binding on everyone is lost."[16] This in turn creates conflict and destabilization in communities: "If the promotion of the self is understood in terms of absolute autonomy, people inevitably reach the point of rejecting one another [and] society becomes a mass of individuals placed side by side, but without any mutual bonds." The collapse of moral consensus ultimately makes it impossible to maintain the common life of communities or to realize the common good.

Today some Catholic public officials seem unable to appreciate these concerns. For more than thirty years some have said that while they are personally opposed to abortion, they will not impose their view on others. They say they do not oppose the view of their church on abortion; they simply believe that it should not have general application, or at least any application supported by law.

These are thoughtful legislators who take their work seriously. It is difficult to understand why, while they are often outspoken about the need to retain the right to abortion, they remain silent about the reason for their own personal opposition to abortion. Catholics who assert they are "personally opposed" to abortion never seem to find the opportunity to tell us—or, more important, to tell young women—why they consider abortion to be a bad choice. Who knows how many abortions could have been avoided and how many lives saved if politicians who refuse to vote for legal restrictions on abortion would at least speak out against its practice?

This silence is increasingly untenable within the Catholic community. It is untenable because it runs counter to the renewal of the Church begun by the Second Vatican Council. This renewal is about a right ordering between faith and reason that leads to an integrated Christian witness on the part of every Catholic. Nothing could be further from the idea of the Second Vatican Council to renew society than the claim that one's moral position on issues of social justice is a matter of private concern, not public conviction. It simply is incoherent to say one agrees that abortion is the killing of an innocent human being—as the Catholic Church recognizes—and then maintain that the law should recognize a "right" to engage in such killing.

Some Catholic politicians who dissent from the Church's views on abortion have cited St. Thomas More (1478–1535) as a role model. I have never understood why they identify with More. He gave up his career, and ultimately his life, in defense of the teaching of the church, not in opposition to it.

Today Thomas More is recognized as one of the great defenders of human dignity and the rights of human conscience. More had gained considerable fame and fortune as a lawyer in Tudor England. He became a great favorite of King Henry VIII, who bestowed generous grants of land on him and made him chancellor of England in 1529. But More's tenure on this pinnacle was short-lived, coinciding as it did with Henry's break with the Catholic Church. Henry was married to Catherine of Aragon, but their union produced only one daughter. Henry, preoccupied with securing his own successor through a male heir, wanted his marriage to Catherine annulled. For this he needed a papal dispensation, which the pope refused to grant.

The next five years were marked by a widening rift between Henry and the Catholic Church, which culminated in Parliament's passing of the Act of Supremacy in March 1534. The act asserted that "the King's Majesty justly and rightfully is and ought to be the supreme head of the Church of England."[17] The measure also required English subjects to take an oath acknowledging the offspring of Henry and his new queen, Anne Boleyn, as the legitimate heir to the throne—thus acknowledging the legitimacy of Henry's divorce.

During this period, More, while making every effort to avoid a confrontation with the king, remained firmly on the side of the Church. The Act of Succession imposed a fatal choice on him: he could either take the oath or risk indictment for treason. Choosing the second option, he was imprisoned in the Tower of London in April 1534. While in prison, More was subjected to pressure from all sides to change his mind, but he steadfastly refused. Finally, on July 1, 1535, he was formally charged with treason. He was promptly found guilty and was beheaded on July 6, 1535. Exactly four hundred years later, More was canonized by Pope Pius XI. Simply yet profoundly, More set the standard for all those of the Christian faith who serve in government when he said just before his execution, "Tell the King, I die the King's loyal servant, but God's first."

Everything we know about More tells us that he cared deeply for his family. One reason he sought so desperately to avoid a confrontation with the king was to protect them. Yet finally More was to sacrifice both his life and his family's security for a principle that gave an eternal meaning and an eternal unity to his family: the sacramental nature of marriage. For in agreeing to the dissolution of the king's marriage, there was also an implicit agreement to the possible dissolution of *any* marriage. This was a point that could not have been lost on a lawyer of More's brilliance. Thus one of history's great statesmen and men of conscience went to his death for a principled defense of the sacramental unity of marriage.

Clarence Miller, one of the editors of the *Complete Works of St. Thomas More*, enumerates what scholars give as the various grounds for More's martyrdom: "the integrity of the self as witnessed by an oath, the irreducible freedom of the individual conscience in the face of an authoritarian state, papal supremacy as a sign of the supra-national unity of Western Christendom, past and present." Then Miller writes, "All of these are true as far as they go. But in the last analysis More did not die for any principle, or idea, or tradition, or even doctrine, but for a person, for Christ. As Bolt makes More say in the play: 'Well . . . finally . . . it isn't a matter of reason; finally it's a matter of love.'"[18]

After so many years, it is perhaps too easy to view the English Catholic martyrs of the sixteenth century as displaying almost an eagerness for their fate. The following passage written by More while he was in the Tower reveals something very different. In *De Tristitia Christi* ("On the Sorrow of Christ"), More wrote of the martyr's encounter with Christ, who says this to his follower:

> You are afraid, you are sad, you are stricken with weariness and dread of the torment with which you have been cruelly threatened. Trust me. I conquered the world, and yet I suffered immeasurably more from fear. I was sadder, more afflicted with weariness, more horrified at the prospect of such cruel suffering drawing eagerly nearer and nearer. Let the brave man have his high-spirited martyrs, let him rejoice

in imitating of them. But you, my timorous and feeble little sheep, be content to have me alone as your shepherd, follow my leadership; if you do not trust yourself, place your trust in me. See, I am walking ahead of you along this fearful road.[19]

More teaches us that for the Catholic, government service opens the possibility of martyrdom. Certainly this was the case in More's time and throughout the sixteenth century. It was equally true throughout much of the twentieth century. It remains true in our own day. Politics too often is the arena of personal self-promotion. But for a Catholic, government service is a vocation—a following of Christ that may be open to martyrdom—if not a bloody martyrdom, then a martyrdom of career and reputation. Catholic politicians who say they are "personally opposed" to abortion but refuse to oppose it in the public arena are not like More. They are more like the Catholics in England who sided with Henry VIII. Like Thomas Cromwell and Thomas Cranmer, these politicians usually find their careers advanced by opposition to their church.

Mother Teresa of Calcutta personified the Gospel of life not only in her unrelenting service to the poor but also in her outspoken defense of the right to life. In the speech she delivered when receiving the Nobel Peace Prize in 1979, she said, "I feel the greatest destroyer of peace today is abortion, because it is a direct war, a direct killing—direct murder by the mother herself. And we read in the Scripture, for God says very clearly: Even if a mother could forget her child—I will not forget you—I have carved you in the palm of my hand."[20] She repeated the same idea in Washington, D.C., in front of the president when she spoke at the National Prayer Breakfast. In her work and in her life, Mother Teresa made it abundantly clear that there is only one Gospel of life. And she was not afraid to say to politicians that there was not a different Gospel of life for those in government.

Pope John Paul II stood steadfastly for the same values throughout his pontificate, urging Catholics to be "a people of life and a people for life."[21] He insisted that every society must acknowledge the three fundamental principles of the culture of life. The first is the incomparable value and dignity of every human being regardless of age, condition, or race. This is especially true in the case of the poor, the weak, and the defenseless. The second is that it is always a violation of human dignity to treat anyone as an instrument or means to an end. Instead, every person must be seen as good in himself or herself and never as an object to be manipulated. The third principle is that the intentional killing of an innocent human being, whatever the circumstances and particularly in cases of abortion and euthanasia, cannot be morally justified.

By insisting that the Catholic people must be "a people of life and a people for life," John Paul II outlined the mission of the Catholic people in the conversion of culture. In this way, Catholics will bear witness to truth, to conscience, and to the possibility of building a culture of life. For him, "The Gospel of God's love for man, the Gospel of the dignity of the person and the Gospel of life are a single and indivisible Gospel."[22]

SUGGESTIONS FOR CONTEMPLATION AND ACTION

1. Think back to a time in your life when you felt called upon to risk something—your friends, your job, your social status—for something you thought was right. How willing were you to make this sacrifice? Did you do it?

2. Take some time reflecting on the things that are dear to you in life: your home, your family, your position in life. Then consider what principles you believe in strongly enough to risk these things for. In all honesty, would you

be able to put your possessions, your family, your life in jeopardy for what you truly believe in?

3. The culture of death, as defined in this chapter, essentially says that human beings are dispensable; they can be used as means rather than as ends. For the next week, look for evidence of this attitude in the media and in the society around you. Decide for yourself whether we are moving closer toward a culture of death. What might you do to help society move toward a culture of life?

4. Take an individual you know—either personally or in history—whom you admire for standing up on behalf of a moral position. What traits do you most admire in this person? How did he or she manage to give conscience a voice? How might you be able to do the same for your own conscience? Think of one or two ways in which you could become more like this person, and try to put them into practice.

9

A Continent of Baptized Christians

Several years ago, I led a delegation of Knights of Columbus to the Basilica of Our Lady of Guadalupe in Monterrey, Mexico, on her feast day. During the celebration of the Mass, I was given an unusual place of honor—a chair behind the main altar—so that I was facing the congregation and watching the back of the cardinal archbishop as he celebrated the Mass.

As the celebrant began the Eucharistic prayer, a poor Mexican mother carrying a tiny infant in her arms began to move down the center aisle on her knees. She proceeded up the stairs to the altar and, placing her child on the floor just in front of the altar, folded her hands and began to pray as the cardinal elevated the host at the consecration. Since that time I have often thought of this woman with her child, facing me at the opposite side of the altar, as a metaphor for the situation of Catholics in the Western Hemisphere. And I have never once doubted which of us had the real place of honor in the heavenly banquet that was celebrated that day.

Many religions have viewed wealth and physical possessions as distractions from the spiritual life and spiritual values. Jesus also makes this point when he reminds us that "where your treasure is, there will your heart be also."[1] Therefore he commands, "Sell what you have, and give to the poor, and you will have treasure in heaven."[2] But Jesus has done something more. He has identified himself personally with the poor, with their condition and with their suffering. At the Last Judgment, he says, his followers will ask him, "Lord, when did we see thee hungry and feed thee, or thirsty and give thee drink?" And he will reply, "Truly, I say to you, as you did it to one of the least of these my brethren, you did it to me." Those who did not obey him will ask, "Lord, when did we see thee hungry or thirsty or a stranger or naked or sick or in prison, and did not minister to thee?" And he will reply: "Truly, I say to you, as you did it not to one of the least of these, you did it not to me."[3]

Indeed from the moment of his birth, Jesus displayed a divine solidarity with the poor. There was no room for him in the inn. His first bed was a manger fit only for animals. Later his family had to flee from persecution and was forced to live in exile in Egypt. As John Paul II has written:

> In Jesus, God came seeking human hospitality. This is why he makes the willingness to welcome others in love a characteristic virtue of believers. He chose to be born into a family that found no lodging in Bethlehem and experienced exile in Egypt. Jesus, who "had nowhere to lay his head," asked those he met for hospitality. To Zacchaeus he said: "I must stay at your house today." He even compared himself to a foreigner in need of shelter: "I was a stranger and you welcomed me." In sending his disciples out on mission, Jesus makes the hospitality they will enjoy an act that concerns him personally: "He who receives you receives me, and he who receives me receives him who sent me."[4]

Mother Teresa emphasized these truths often when she told us to "take time to love Jesus in the poor." Mother Teresa worked chiefly with the poor in Calcutta, most of whom had little or no experience of Christianity. Her ministry—like the message of the

Good Samaritan—makes it clear that Christian charity cannot be limited by race, faith, or nationality.

These messages are all familiar. We can see how the call to "love Jesus in the poor" urges us to remember the divine presence in every individual, no matter how disadvantaged, when we pass that person on the street. But how are we to apply this message collectively, when it is a matter not of one individual but of an entire nation that is more affluent, prosperous, and powerful than another?

All this presents a special challenge to those of us living in affluence in the United States who are surrounded by extreme poverty in Asia, Africa, and Latin America. It is still more pressing when we reflect that many of those who are suffering from want are Christians. The global community of Christians is overwhelmingly poor, and this trend will probably continue throughout the twenty-first century. In his book *The Next Christendom*, Philip Jenkins, professor of religious studies at Pennsylvania State University, writes.

> Considering Christianity as a global reality can make us see the whole religion in a radically new perspective, which is startling and, often, uncomfortable.... Christianity is deeply associated with poverty. Contrary to myth, the typical Christian is not a White fat cat in the United States or western Europe, but rather a poor person, often unimaginably poor by Western standards.[5]

Population trends projected for the next several decades suggest the potential for even greater disparity as the percentage of world Catholics (and Christians as a whole) living in the poorer Southern Hemisphere continues to increase. Jenkins suggests that by 2020, Africans and Latin Americans combined will make up 60 percent of all Catholics.[6] By 2050, it is expected that the following nations will have more than 100 million Catholics:

Brazil, Mexico, the Philippines, the United States, Nigeria, and Zaire/Congo.

The church of the future will be not only increasingly poor but increasingly *young*. As we have seen, the church is growing most rapidly in the Southern Hemisphere, and in these nations the proportion of people under the age of fourteen is much higher than it is in the Northern Hemisphere. In Europe, only some 16–20 percent of the population is under fourteen, whereas in the global South, the figure is closer to one third—and in some cases is much higher.[7]

Most of us in the United States have not thoroughly considered the implications of these realities. But this does not make the challenges they present to Christian solidarity any less real. The vast gulf between the church of the affluent and the church of the poor cries out for a new commitment to global solidarity. In *Deus Caritas Est* Pope Benedict XVI wrote, "The Church is God's family in the world. In this family no one ought to go without the necessities of life."[8] The sad reality is that millions in this family suffer each day without these necessities.

One extraordinary response to this need was the 1997 Special Assembly for America of the Synod of Bishops. Its theme was "The Encounter with the Living Christ: The Way to Conversion, Communion, and Solidarity in America." Pope John Paul II had called for the synod, or assembly of church officials, as part of five special synods, one for each continent. For the Western Hemisphere, he chose to speak not of the "Americas," but of "America" in the singular, in order to emphasize "all that is common to the peoples of the continent, including their shared Christian identity and their genuine attempt to strengthen the bonds of solidarity and communion between the different forms of the continent's rich cultural heritage."[9]

The Synod for America is one of the most important events for the future of the Catholic Church. Although in many places its work has unfortunately been forgotten, its promise remains great, especially as the church in Latin America continues to gain importance. Whether the synod's promise can still be achieved will depend on whether Catholics in the United States can take up its challenge to transcend national boundaries in the work of charity and justice throughout the Western Hemisphere and ultimately around the globe. In this respect, the synod states:

> The field of social structures is another area for conversion. Certain economic systems and policies exist which control the commercial market and affect the financial matter of loans and interests, generating in some cases an enormous debt for nations and impeding the development of peoples. There are also certain types of economic aid dependent on the ideologies of small political groups, various people in power and nations which are not always governed by the criteria of equity and solidarity, but rather by selfish interests. Such conditions call for conversion, especially as they relate to the economic inequality between the northern and southern areas of the continent. The situation calls out to faith and to conscience—both human and Christian—for a response.[10]

As this passage suggests, the issues we have been examining in this book are more interrelated than they may first seem. One component of the "economic inequality" that is lying in the background of so many of our current problems is, quite simply, "selfish interests." Ethical business practices cannot be based upon oppression and injustice inflicted on people, even if those people are far off in other nations. Those who indulge their selfish interests may have many forms of rationalization for their actions—arguments that cultural conditions are different in those countries, that exploited workers are better off than they might otherwise be—but rationalizations are not valid reasons

Where does the remedy lie? The quickest and surest solution would be if everyone were to live and act according to the ethics of the Gospels. This answer may sound either sanctimonious or idealistic, but it is true. It would be impossible to ignore an individual's suffering if one were capable of seeing Christ in him or her. It would be impossible to exploit one's neighbor if one truly loved him as oneself. As we have already seen, laws and regulations are mere (but regrettably necessary) stand-ins for the lack of love in the human heart. And yet, this is precisely the Christian challenge. In a sermon given in 1964, Father Joseph Ratzinger said this:

> For love, as it is here portrayed as the content of being a Christian, demands that we try to live as God lives. He loves us, not because we are especially good, particularly virtuous, or of any great merit, not because we are useful or even necessary to him; he loves us not because *we* are good, but because *he* is good. . . . To love in the Christian sense means trying to follow in this path.[11]

This issue lies at the center of today's world problems. They certainly seem diverse—economic inequalities, environmental destruction, terrorism, war—so diverse, in fact, that it is hard to imagine a single answer that would resolve them all. And yet there *is* a single answer. All of these problems are ramifications of one great issue in our time: human ethical development has not kept pace with intellectual and technological development. We now have capacities that far exceed the imaginations of even the most farsighted visionaries of a hundred years ago. Yet we remain as stymied by greed, hatred, and violence as ever. Christianity has always taught that we live in a fallen world and we cannot expect perfection from it, but even so, we still have a great deal of leeway in our ethical choices. Until our moral development catches up with our progress in other areas, many of the problems we face today will continue to be irresolvable. The synod acknowledged this fact when it asserted that its discussions and recommendations "will not have a sociological or technical emphasis, but one based on the Gospel."[12]

One of the greatest tests of whether the Catholic Church is ready to help the nations of the Western Hemisphere move toward greater ethical maturity will involve our ability to integrate Hispanic Catholics into the Catholic community and then into the larger society within the United States. The success of this effort will likely determine the future of Catholicism in the United States and in much of the Western Hemisphere. Since 1960, more than 70 percent of the growth in the Catholic Church in the United States has been due to the growth of the Hispanic population. Today, 39 percent of American Catholics are Hispanic.[13] In the not too distant future, the majority of Catholics in the United States will be of Hispanic heritage. The Synod for America conveyed a genuinely Catholic message to "immigrants who find yourselves unwelcome in the lands where you have moved. . . . The Church has walked alongside generations of migrants in the march for a better life, and she will not cease to stand by you with every kind of service."[14]

The struggle for integration of immigrant Catholics into the American mainstream is far from new. In 1854, Pope Pius IX sent a gift to the American people: a stone from the ancient Roman Temple of Concord. The pope intended that the stone be included in the monument that was being built in the nation's capital in honor of its first president. It was a mark of the anti-Catholicism of the times that rumors soon began to spread that placement of the stone in the Washington Monument would be the signal for a Catholic coup that would turn the nation's government over to the pope. And so, in the dead of night on March 6, 1854, a group of men stole the stone, and either smashed it into small pieces or threw it into the Potomac River. The men who had "saved" the republic that evening were Know-Nothings, a political party dedicated to opposing the influence of Catholics in American society and politics. Their platform included prohibiting Catholics from holding public office on the grounds that they owed allegiance to a "foreign prince," that is, the pope.

During the congressional elections that year, the Know-Nothings elected more than a hundred of their members to the United States Congress. In order to continue their "rescue" mission, the Know-Nothings took over control of the Monument Society that was entrusted with the building of the Washington Monument with money appropriated by the Congress. Soon Congress cut off funds for the project, and construction came to a halt. It would be more than two decades before the project was resumed. When it did, stone from the original quarry was unavailable, and stone from a new quarry had to be found. That is why, on a bright sunny day in Washington, you can see that almost halfway up the monument the color of the stone changes.

We have come a long way from the rabid anti-Catholicism of those times. In 1928, Al Smith was nominated for the presidency by the Democratic Party—the first Catholic to be nominated for this office by a major party. In 1960 John F. Kennedy became the first, and so far only, Catholic to be elected to the highest office in the land. In both of these elections, some individuals expressed concerns about the supposed dangers of electing a Catholic to the presidency. Since Kennedy's presidency, there have continued to be many Catholic politicians of widely divergent ideologies. No observers of the political scene, however—none, at any rate, in the mainstream of American thought—doubt these politicians' essential loyalty to this country.

Fears of an imagined Catholic fifth column or the alleged subservience of American Catholics to a "foreign prince" are, for the overwhelming majority of Americans, a thing of the past. Consequently, those of us who now live in great comfort in the United States sometimes too easily forget the abject poverty and desperate circumstances that drove our ancestors to come to America—

and the prejudice and suspicion that often met them when they arrived. We may ask ourselves how we, in turn, are greeting today's newcomers.

American Catholics bring a unique perspective to our country's relationship with Latin America, since it is populated largely by fellow Catholics, our brothers and sisters in Christ. When the bishops of the hemisphere met at the Synod for America, they articulated a view that invited us all to adopt a revolutionary rethinking of the way we view one another: "We believe that we are one community; and, although America comprises many nations, cultures and languages, there is so much that links us together and so many ways in which each of us affects the lives of our neighbors."[15] Latin America's Catholic roots are obvious, and the United States shares those same roots in Florida and the Southwest. Maryland, Louisiana, Quebec, and the Maritime Provinces round out this heritage in the United States and Canada. Each nation in North America has a deep-rooted common spiritual heritage.

There can be little doubt that ours is, in the words of Pope Benedict, "a continent of baptized Christians." More precisely, it is a continent where the majority of persons are baptized Catholics. Our goal should be to create a vibrant (North, Central, and South) American Catholic community in which our shared faith and values become a light to the entire world. But we can hardly do so if we view immigrants from elsewhere in the hemisphere with suspicion and hostility. Indeed for Catholics, immigration brings a unique benefit. Hispanic immigration holds out the promise of a revitalization of our parishes. It is up to the Catholics already in the United States to provide a rich spiritual environment that will feed the needs of these new arrivals. As these immigrants breathe new life into parish communities, it is our job to help them assimilate into our parishes and communities, as our parents and grandparents did, and to help them to live their faith with support from all Catholics.

Speaking at the Shrine of Aparecida in 2007, Pope Benedict provided criteria in undertaking this task from the cultural viewpoint. He stated:

> Authentic cultures are not closed in upon themselves, nor are they set in stone at a particular point in history, but they are open, or better still, they are seeking an encounter with other cultures, hoping to reach universality through encounter and dialogue with other ways of life and with elements that can lead to a new synthesis, in which diversity of expressions is always respected as well as the diversity of their particular cultural embodiment.[16]

Robert A. Pastor, writing in *Newsweek*, points out that "roughly 90 percent of all Mexican illegal immigrants leave jobs to come to the United States; they seek higher wages. Illegal immigration is not likely to shrink until the income gap begins to narrow."[17] Pastor suggests that the North American nations need to "think in more regional terms." He points out that there were similar concerns about immigration in the European Community (now called the European Union, or EU) when it accepted Greece, Spain, Portugal, and Ireland as members—all of which had per-capita income that was significantly lower than the EU as a whole. When these nations were admitted in the 1980s, the EU channeled some $500 billion in aid to them. As a result, "between 1986 and 2003, the per-capita gross domestic product (GDP) of the four nations rose from 65 percent of the average EU member country's economic output to 82 percent. Spain spent much of the $120 billion it received on new roads that boosted commerce and tourism. As a result, Spanish immigration to other European countries all but ceased. Ireland now ranks as the second richest member of the EU in per-capita terms—and for the first time in its history, it is actually receiving rather than sending immigrants."

North America is not Europe, but it might benefit from considering Europe's example. Pastor suggests:

> The first thing NAFTA [North American Free Trade Agreement] partners should do is establish a North American Investment Fund that would invest $200 billion in 10 years in roads and communications connecting the poorer southern part of Mexico to the North American market. If we build them, they will stay: companies will be more likely to invest there, encouraging many Mexican workers to stay home and others, already in the United States, to return.[18]

We could easily debate specific figures and proposals, but in essence the solution is clear: we will not resolve the immigration issue unless we remedy the tremendous economic inequity between the United States and its southern neighbors. All this is to stress that we should have more engagement with Mexico and Latin America, not less. Catholics on both sides of the border must take the initiative to promote a Catholic solution to the problems of poverty and to promote economic and educational opportunities for the poor of the region. This is a special responsibility of Catholics in the United States—especially leaders in business and finance—and we should not wait for political solutions in order to begin this engagement.

On the other hand, engagement is not a unilateral process. The economic imbalances between the United States and its southern neighbors cannot be solved simply by throwing money at the problem. With the notable exceptions of Costa Rica and Chile, much of Latin America has failed to make the necessary economic and political reforms that would make possible the kind of economic growth experienced in Ireland and Spain. Catholics in Mexico and the United States have every reason to work for a day when such close neighbors are even closer friends.

When I served as a member of the White House staff in the 1980s, I spent considerable time working on President Reagan's change of American foreign policy regarding the United Nations International Conference on Population. The meeting held in Mexico City in 1984 considered the relationship between population growth and economic development. At that time I became convinced that many Third World governments that could not create jobs or improve living standards because of political corruption or stagnant government-planned economies were quick to blame their own population for their problems. These governments implemented extensive family-planning programs while leaving in place structures that restricted political and economic initiative. President Reagan's view was that for some governments population control became an easy way of avoiding responsibility for the difficult issues that were the fundamental reasons for widespread poverty. More than twenty years later, the same tendency remains. Despite some successes, such as the emergence of an effective multiparty political system, Mexico has not yet been able to make substantial economic reforms. People are still viewed as a problem, but migration is the new answer.

The message of the Synod for America cuts both ways. There is a definite responsibility for the United States, but there are also responsibilities for our neighbors to the south. The immigration problem will not be solved without a serious improvement in the infrastructure of the Latin American nations. But infrastructure means not only roads and utilities but the far more crucial foundation of a national commitment to the rule of law—of honest government, freedom from corruption, and real economic opportunity for the poor. There is a clear and urgent need for economic and political reform.

The outcome of the immigration issue is of utmost importance for the Catholic Church in this hemisphere and indeed throughout the world. Many of us continue to think of Christianity as it was in the past: centered in Europe, with outposts in the Ameri-

cas and little more than a missionary presence in Africa and Asia.
All this has changed over the past half century. In terms of population, the center of the Catholic Church has shifted dramatically
from the North to the South; Latin America alone currently accounts for 42 percent of the world's Catholics. It might surprise
many to learn that there are already more Catholic baptisms in
the Philippines each year than in the four largest Catholic nations
in Europe—Italy, France, Spain, and Poland—combined.[19]

Philip Jenkins writes: "Europe . . . notionally has a present-day
Christian population of 560 million. To say the least, that number
looks optimistic. Over the past century or so, massive secularization has seriously reduced the population of European Christians,
whether we judge 'Christianity' by general self-definition, or else
demand evidence of practice and commitment."[20] In reality, the
number of active and practicing Catholics in countries such as
France and Italy now ranges from around 8 to 10 percent of the
population.[21]

The juridical center of the Catholic Church, of course, remains
in Rome, and the intellectual center is still for the most part in
Europe. But unless a reevangelization takes hold in Europe
quickly to counter that continent's pervasive and deepening secularization, there will be significant changes in the not too distant
future. As we look to the future, we can see a growing global
Catholic community of approximately one billion persons, mostly
in the Western Hemisphere, but also significantly in Asia and
Africa, facing the emerging economic and political influence of
more than one billion Muslims, and India's and China's populations of more than one billion people each—many of whom are
more or less indifferent to Christianity and an untold number
hostile to it. From a geopolitical, or rather georeligious, standpoint, this development more than justifies the many pastoral
visits Pope John Paul II made to Africa, Asia, and Latin America.
But this trend also has serious implications for the United States.
Statistics indicate that the United States will remain a country in

which the majority of the population identify themselves as Christians. Certainly, then, much more is at stake in our long debate over Hispanic immigration policy than rising levels of government expenditures for health, education, welfare, and border security—as important as those subjects are.

In the five hundred years since Columbus landed in the New World, America's culture has been viewed as essentially dependent upon European culture and during much of that time dependent on English culture. Demographic trends during the past several decades clearly suggest that this phase is coming to an end. But if American culture will in the future be less derivative of European culture, what *will* it be an expression of? Catholics may hope that part of the answer may be found in the influence and promise of an event in Catholic history nearly as old as the landing of Christopher Columbus in the New World. In 1999, John Paul II wrote:

> The appearance of Mary to the native Juan Diego on the hill of Tepeyac in 1531 had a decisive effect on evangelization. Its influence greatly overflows the boundaries of Mexico, spreading to the whole continent. America, which historically has been, and still is, a melting-pot of peoples, has recognized in the *mestiza* face of the Virgin of Tepeyac, "in Blessed Mary of Guadalupe, an impressive example of a perfectly inculturated evangelization." Consequently, not only in Central and South America, but in North America as well, the Virgin of Guadalupe is venerated as Queen of all America.[22]

It would be too simplistic to see in the *mestiza* face of the Virgin Mary's appearance a new, mixed race of peoples. But it would not be simplistic at all to perceive in that *mestiza* face and in her message to a Native American the promise of a new *culture*—a culture informed by a Christian idea and sensibility experienced in the

Western Hemisphere during nearly five centuries. Many Catholics in the United States now venerate Our Lady of Guadalupe as patroness of a new culture of life. Why should that culture not transcend national borders? And why should a culture of life not also be a culture of unity and inclusion?

Our entire continent has been uniquely blessed by the Mother of God. Mary, through her image left on St. Juan Diego's tilma, has called millions to conversion in the Americas in the greatest conversion to Catholicism in history. And that conversion is still continuing. Of Our Lady of Guadalupe, Pope Benedict XIV wrote: "To no other nation has such a wonder been done." At the time he wrote those words in 1754, that *nation* stretched from the San Juan Islands north of Seattle through Central America. Thus two centuries later, Pope Pius XII accurately proclaimed Our Lady of Guadalupe "Empress of the Americas." The wonder that had been done was for all the people of our continent. Because of Our Lady of Guadalupe, our Church faces a bright future on this continent. No other place on earth has as many practicing Catholics as the Americas.

Given the increasing secularization of Europe and the growth of the Catholic community in the Western Hemisphere, these questions must be asked: How will the shifting demographic center of world Catholicism affect intellectual and cultural realities in our hemisphere in the future? Will the Catholicism of the Western—the Christian—Hemisphere be able to resist the European trend toward secularization? Today no one can say for sure. But what is already certain is that the changing demographics of world Catholicism now impose tremendous responsibilities on Catholics in the United States. Just as the United States cannot regard itself as economically isolated from the rest of the hemisphere, American Catholics cannot limit their cultural and intellectual perspective to their customary Eurocentric horizons. At this point, the future of the Catholic Church in this nation is intimately and irrevocably linked with the future of the Hispanic

people. If this is so, and if the possibility of building a culture of life
in the United States can only be recognized through the efforts of a
growing community of Catholics who are themselves committed
to being "a people of life and a people for life," then it is also true
that the future prospects of a culture of life in our country are in-
separably tied to the future of Hispanics in America.

There are more than 150 million Catholics living throughout
North America. Are not the spiritual and sacramental ties that
unite them greater than those of economics and trade? The experience of the 1.5 million members of the Knights of Columbus
living in North America is that our spiritual unity has deep roots
and offers great promise for the future. In less than twenty-five
years from its founding in 1882, the Knights of Columbus was
active in both Canada and Mexico and had a long tradition of
cooperation across our national borders.

One example of how this has worked in real life is the van der
Zalm family. Ted van der Zalm started working as a missionary in
Africa in the 1980s. While serving there, he met his future wife,
Miriam. "I had been praying for someone to spend my life with,"
Ted recalled. On his way home, during a stopover in Amsterdam,
he had a revelation and realized, "This is the girl God wanted me
to marry." He bought a ring, traveled to Italy (her native country),
and asked her to marry him. He had to work to convince her parents that he was the right man for her, but finally the couple
became engaged.

Eventually both Ted and Miriam finished their missionary
work and settled in Niagara, Ontario, where they had a successful
greenhouse business. Ted joined the Knights of Columbus and is
now the father of five young children. But Ted was not satisfied
with his new profession. "I felt you don't stay ten years in Africa
to spend the rest of your life growing house plants," he said.

Several years ago the van der Zalms read a United Nations
report that stated that a person dies every eight seconds be-

cause of water-related diseases. They decided to do something about the problem. In the fall of 2004, they mortgaged their house in Ontario in order to purchase well-digging equipment and founded an organization called Wells of Hope. With their new equipment, they and their children drove from Canada to Guatemala. Local Knights of Columbus councils helped provide the van der Zalms with meals, lodging, and gas money along the way.

The work has brought its share of sacrifices. In one instance, Ted spent over three weeks digging a well by hand, eventually making a hole that went seventy-five feet down, although it was only two feet wide. There was no shoring, and he had to be lowered down on a rope. In the process, he lost the sight in one eye from dehydration and exhaustion.

Nonetheless, Ted feels that God is helping their efforts. "I can't tell you how often I meet the right people, or received help exactly when it was needed," he says.[23] Ted and Miriam's efforts to provide irrigation and safe drinking water in rural Guatemala have saved hundreds, perhaps thousands, of lives already.

It is not hard to find in Ted and Miriam and their children a "community of persons" joined in love, but it is not a love that keeps to itself. Devoting themselves to service to life in a highly practical and down-to-earth fashion, the van der Zalms are making a powerful impact on society, and in this way they are serving the church and her mission in the world. In his *Letter to Families,* John Paul II insisted that "the civilization of love is possible; it is not a utopia."[24] The van der Zalms are each day proving that in this way, too, John Paul II was prophetic. They represent a new form of Christian solidarity for the twenty-first century—one that finds personal ways to transcend national barriers in helping the poor. They are one family proving that "The Church is God's family in the world."

Suggestions for Contemplation and Action

1. Recollect what you know of your own family history. When did your ancestors come to the United States? What do you know about the reasons they had for coming?

2. Reflect on the many identities you have as an individual: religious, national, regional, and universal. Which of these is the most important to you? How does one identity affect another? Do you feel you have a higher loyalty to one type of identity than to the others?

3. For the next week make a point of noticing your responses to people of various ethnic groups, whether you see them in person or through the media. How automatic are your responses? Are your attitudes justified by your own past experience? Do you find you are filtering your experiences to jibe with your prejudices?

4. The next time you find yourself irritated with someone— say, at being jostled in a store or cut off in traffic—notice your responses. Does anger come up immediately? If so, how do you deal with it? If the person who irritates you is from another race or nationality, do you find yourself jumping to conclusions about "those people"?

5. Sometime in the next week, take at least one concrete action to help the poor. It may include volunteering time to a charitable organization, making a donation to such an organization, or even giving a gift to an individual. Notice your internal reactions to this practice. Are you really giving out of kindness or compassion? Does it feel like a duty? Do you resent or begrudge what you are giving? Pay particular attention to any thoughts you have about whether the person you are helping "deserves" it or not.

Conclusion

On October 7, 1979, I stood on the grass of the Mall in Washington, D.C., with hundreds of thousands of other Catholics to join John Paul II as he said Mass for the last time on his first visit to the United States. I still remember clearly the sky beginning to darken, the pope's green vestments blowing in the wind, his hand resting on his silver pilgrim's cross, the Capitol dome behind him; and then the heavily accented Polish voice that would grow so familiar as the years went on:

> All human beings ought to value every person for his or her uniqueness as a creature of God, called to be a brother or sister of Christ. . . . And so, we will stand up every time that human life is threatened. When the sacredness of life before birth is attacked, we will stand up and proclaim that no one ever has the authority to destroy unborn life.[1]

And then he went on, repeating his refrain, saying we would stand up to protect children, marriage, the family, the environment, the poor, and finally, "When the sick, the aged or the dying are abandoned in loneliness, we will stand up and proclaim that they are worthy of love, care and respect."[2]

Of course, we were all *standing*.

John Paul II changed my life that day, although at the time, I did not know how much. All I did know was that nothing again would be quite the same.

Before coming to the Mall, John Paul had granted a vastly smaller and private audience: he met the officers and directors of the Knights of Columbus to thank them personally for what he said was "your solidarity with the mission of the pope"[3] and to encourage their work of evangelization and charity. At the time, I did not even know the meeting had occurred. I was not yet a member of the Knights of Columbus; there was no Knights of Columbus council in the parish I attended. But this meeting, too, in the logic of providence, would ultimately affect my future.

Fifteen months later, I was in Rome to speak at an international conference on family life. It was an occasion to personally meet John Paul II. Soon after that I returned to Rome, invited to meet with him privately in the papal residence to provide further details on some of the issues I had spoken about at that family conference. After that, for nearly twenty-five years, I had the privilege of engaging in similar meetings with John Paul II on the themes he had spoken of that afternoon on the Mall: the nature of marriage and the family and the value of human life.

Shortly after that first meeting with John Paul II, a good friend gave me a copy of a book written just after the Second Vatican Council by a German theologian who had attended that meeting and whom the pope had recently brought to Rome to serve as prefect of one of the Vatican congregations. My friend was the one person I knew in the United States who seemed to have a clear idea of what John Paul II was trying to do and why. He said the book was must reading. Its title is *Introduction to Christianity*; the author, Joseph Ratzinger (now Pope Benedict XVI). It dealt with a subject I thought I had already been introduced to, and so I promptly put the gift on a bookshelf at home, which is where it stayed for months. One weekend I finally started reading this "introduction." But if this book was an *introduction*, then it was the type someone would make at a university doctoral students' seminar.

Chapter 1 addressed the "question of God" and the problem of belief in the modern world with its almost overwhelming sense of doubt. Ratzinger wrote that for the believer to say "Amen" to the Christian revelation means to "take one's stand on something, believe in something; thus faith in God appears as a holding on to God through which man gains a firm hold for his life. Faith is thereby defined as taking up a position, as taking a stand trustfully on the ground of the word of God."[4] And then a little later, "For to believe as a Christian means in fact entrusting oneself to the meaning that bears upon me and the world; taking it as the firm ground on which I can stand fearlessly."[5] Of course, this "ground" is not a philosophical or political abstraction; it is a person—Jesus of Nazareth.

Reading these words, I thought again of the Mass on the Mall years earlier. To "believe" as a Christian is to "stand trustfully," to "stand fearlessly"—to stand up.

It had been easy to hear the words of John Paul II in Washington and to understand that what he said had a political meaning. It was little more than five years since the Supreme Court had decided *Roe v. Wade*; Congress was actively debating the legality of abortion, as were candidates for president such as Ronald Reagan. Catholics were citizens and were called upon to influence—even change—public policy, especially when human lives are at stake. But what the pope had said, Ratzinger's book suggested to me, went far deeper—it was part of the very essence of what it means to be a Christian. "To believe as a Christian," Ratzinger wrote, "means in fact entrusting oneself to the meaning that bears upon me and the world." As I listened more carefully to what John Paul II was saying, it was that this meaning for "me and the world" had a logic, a structure that connected me to the world and to all those in it. It was a structure revealed by the person of Jesus Christ, and because of him this structure was reflected in every person.

This structure is, of course, divine love. Because each human being is called by the Father in love and for love, love is the structure—as John Paul II would say, the vocation—of the human person made in the image of God. Each person is created with the capacity for a loving communion with another person and, therefore, marriage and family is the natural school where this structure is first revealed and this vocation is first learned. Thus, the family is the first cell of society and the basic building block of the civilization of love. John Paul II would say repeatedly that the civilization of love is not a utopia. This is because its foundation is built into the very nature of every family and therefore every society.

John Paul II saw this vocation to love as open to every person regardless of whether he or she is a Christian. But he maintained that the radical meaning of this vocation is revealed most fully through the sacrificial love of Jesus Christ. The gift of self seen most completely in Christ's sacrifice on the cross is the ultimate expression of charity and the criteria by which to ultimately judge human action. Thus, to be a Christian is to radically change one's perception of reality: to see life as a gift, to see one's own self as a gift, and, therefore, to reciprocate by making a gift of self to others.

As Benedict XVI wrote in *Deus Caritas Est*, "We contribute to a better world only by personally doing good now, with full commitment and wherever we have the opportunity, independently of partisan strategies and programs. The Christian's program—the program of the Good Samaritan, the program of Jesus—is 'a heart which sees.' This heart sees where love is needed and acts accordingly."[6] In this book, I have attempted to suggest some implications of how this way of seeing may affect our families, neighbors, communities, businesses, politics, and ultimately our nation and the world.

Two thousand years ago, Jesus said, "My kingdom is not of this world."[7] The night before that pronouncement, he had said of his disciples, "They are not of the world, even as I am not of the world."[8] The question of what Jesus meant still, in a sense, hangs in the air. It expresses a dynamic, even a conflict, that dwells at the heart of Christianity. If Christ's kingdom is not of this world, and we as his followers are not of this world, then what attitude are we to take toward the world?

The answers given even by the most fervent of Christians have varied wildly. For some, like St. Anthony of Egypt, the founder of Christian monasticism, it meant renouncing the world in a very palpable sense. They withdrew from society into a life of solitude and prayer. Others have taken inspiration from another statement of Christ, who said, in praying to the Father, "As thou didst send me into the world, so I have sent them into the world."[9] These Christians have chosen to live a life in the world without being immersed in its concerns and vexations while bearing a living witness to the power of Christ.

The twentieth-century Protestant theologian H. Richard Niebuhr examines these different stances in his classic work *Christ and Culture*. He speaks of three fundamental approaches. First is what he terms the "Christ against culture." Christ's message is understood as meaning a revolt against, or at least a separation from, society, from the "world." Christ's followers are "a new people with a new law." With their moral standards, they set themselves apart from society. According to Niebuhr, examples of this perspective can be found in many of the earliest Christian texts, such as *The Didache* ["Teaching"] *of the Twelve Apostles* or *The Shepherd of Hermas*. Such a view was not surprising in the early days of Christianity. The Roman Empire was not a democratic society. The overwhelming majority of its inhabitants had no say in how they were governed. Any group that wished to live by a different standard of ethics would by necessity have had to see itself as a community apart.

Another advocate of "Christ against culture" was the Russian novelist Leo Tolstoy (1828–1910). Readers of his novels *War and Peace* and, particularly, *Anna Karenina* will remember their constant insistence on the falsity and insincerity of life among the Russian aristocracy. After writing these novels, Tolstoy turned to what he considered to be authentic Christianity, seeking to live solely according to the teachings of the Gospels. Social conventions were unnecessary; money and economics were to be despised.

Such attempts, while undoubtedly high-minded, can prove unrealistic in practice. Tolstoy discovered this truth in his own life. He despised the world of money and gain, but he was also a landowner with large estates. His solution was to leave the management of his property to his wife, who was sorely ill-equipped to handle the job. Tolstoy's estates fell into neglect; one peasant was even buried alive in a sandpit. "I seldom saw father so upset," his daughter later recalled. "'Such things can't happen, they can't happen,' he was telling mother. 'If you want an estate you must manage it well, or else give it up altogether.'"[10] Tolstoy had found he was still in the world.

The second approach that Niebuhr examines is that of the "Christ of culture," in which Christ's teachings are understood as fully compatible with society as conventionally understood. Some philosophers, such as John Locke in his *The Reasonableness of Christianity* or Immanuel Kant in his *Religion within the Limits of Reason Alone*, fall into this category. They reduce Christ to merely a great moral teacher or enlightened peacemaker—someone who essentially fits easily into existing social norms, someone who above all else is reasonable. Thomas Jefferson did something similar in creating a new "gospel." Jefferson cut his Bible apart and pasted down the sections that he felt were true, leaving out the miracles and the Resurrection. The result has come to be known as *The Jefferson Bible*.[11] Jefferson's own title, *The Life and Morals of Jesus of Nazareth*, suggests how Jefferson viewed Christ—solely as an exalted moralist.

The American philosopher William James portrayed something similar in what he called "the religion of healthy-mindedness." For those with this attitude, the world is not essentially problematic or difficult, and the religious person has no trouble fitting in with it. These individuals possess "a temperament organically weighted on the side of cheer and fatally forbidden to linger . . . over the darker aspects of the universe. In some individuals optimism may become quasi-pathological. The capacity for even a transient sadness or a momentary humility seems cut off from them as by a kind of congenital anaesthesia."[12]

What is wrong with this kind of "anaesthesia"? For one thing, it makes compassion virtually impossible. We cannot have compassion without acknowledging the suffering of others. It is hard to imagine Mother Teresa possessing this sort of "healthy-mindedness." There is certainly no value in a morbid obsession with the sorrows of the world, but it is only realistic to recognize that suffering exists—and that it can and must be alleviated with care and compassion.

As Niebuhr himself admits, it can be dangerously simplistic to isolate specific figures or movements into a single category, assuming, for example, that one who withdraws from society has no effects upon it. Niebuhr places Benedictine spirituality in the category of "Christ against culture." It is true that the Benedictines withdrew into their monastic communities, yet they played a tremendous role in shaping the future of Western civilization. Historian Paul Johnson describes the monks' crucial impact on the future of Europe as leaders in agriculture, land improvement, and even accounting: "In a sense they determined the whole future history of Europe: they were the foundation of its world primacy."[13]

Niebuhr goes on to say that in addition to the stances of "Christ against culture" and the "Christ of culture," there is a "Christ above culture." The event of Jesus Christ in history cannot be contained by any individual culture or even by the entirety of human society.

The message and event of Jesus Christ cannot be limited simply to an affirmation—or for that matter, a repudiation—of existing cultural norms. The demand of Christ on the individual believer, the community of Christians, and culture itself cannot be reduced to this level, because the mystery of Christ is incapable of such easy definition. Christ presents a great mystery within history. He at once affirms what is good in a culture and at the same time calls it to an ever-higher level.

Christ presents this "mystery" as the perfect expression of love. He contains in himself both the "duality of the Son of Man and the Son of God, who loves God as man should love Him, and loves man as only God can love. . . . There seems then to be no other adequate way to describe Jesus as having the virtue of love than to say that his love was that of the Son of God. It was not love but God that filled his soul."[14]

Niebuhr understood that while Christ can be seen as affirming the accomplishments of many cultures and in a certain sense as within culture, the Catholic tradition as a whole regards Christ as above culture—as one who is always present to transform culture. This understanding is fundamental in *Evangelium Vitae,* in which John Paul II writes, "The Gospel of life is not simply a reflection, however new and profound, on human life. Nor is it merely a commandment aimed at raising awareness and bringing about significant changes in society. Still less is it an illusory promise of a better future. The Gospel of life is something concrete and personal, for it consists in the proclamation of the very person of Jesus."[15]

This means, at the very least, that the message of Jesus Christ cannot be contained within a single political or economic order. Pope Benedict XVI said as much in *Deus Caritas Est* when he wrote:

Christian charitable activity must be independent of parties and ideologies. It is not a means of changing the world ideologically, and it is not at the service of worldly stratagems, but it is a way of making present here and now the love which man always needs. [16]

In considering the two great cultural interventions of the Christian in the life of society—building a culture of life that respects the sanctity and dignity of every human being, and expressing Christian love through works of charity—Christianity cannot be reduced to another moral, philosophical, or political system, as necessary as Christian activity is in each of these areas. But what is essential, what is foundational, is a personal approach to society's problems based upon the transforming power of Jesus Christ. In his essay *The Idea of a Christian Society*, T. S. Eliot made clear that he was not addressing the question of to what extent a society may profess aspects of the Christian faith or Christian practice or to what extent a society embodies principles of justice or the lack thereof. Instead, he said his concern was with the question of "what—if any—is the 'idea' of the society in which we live? To what end is it arranged?"[17] There are few questions more important today to the future of American society than this one asked by one of America's great poets nearly seventy years ago.

What is at stake from a cultural standpoint is not the imposition of Christianity on society, but expressing a living presence of Christ within society through our personal relationships. Cardinal Joseph Ratzinger, writing shortly before his election as pope, noted: "Our greatest need in the present historical moment is people who make God credible in this world by means of the enlightened faith they live. The negative testimony of Christians who spoke of God but lived in a manner contrary to him has obscured the image of God and has opened the doors to disbelief. We need men who keep their eyes fixed on God, learning from him what true humanity means."[18]

I have often thought that an extraordinary expression of this insight can be seen in the daily work of the millions of members of the Knights of Columbus and their families to implement their principles of charity, unity, and fraternity. Other faith-based associations have also made substantial contributions in this regard, but the Knights of Columbus has been unique in developing a family-centered approach to charity within local communities based upon the special unity of fraternal brotherhood within a Christian ethos.

Elsewhere in the essay quoted above, Cardinal Ratzinger cites the *Rule of St. Benedict* as a principle for the engagement of Christians in contemporary culture: "Let them practice fraternal charity with a pure love." Although St. Benedict crafted his rule to guide the daily lives of monks working and praying behind cloister walls, Cardinal Ratzinger is proposing a startling application of the rule. He is contending that a life of fraternal charity can and should be applied to the lay Christian in the varieties of daily activities. More startling still is the suggestion that the practice of "fraternal charity with a pure love" not only can be applied throughout our personal encounters within the family and the larger society, but is the primary path for building a culture of life and a civilization of love.

During very few periods of history have Catholics confronted such profound and complex challenges as they have in the United States in the past hundred years. These challenges have included industrialization, democracy, immigration, pluralism, bigotry, poverty, and world war. American Catholics have responded faithfully to these challenges, and without the help of king or parliament, they have built a growing and beneficent church community.

The question remains as to what role Catholics are to play in the society of the twenty-first century. Some may express the concern that encouraging Catholics to greater efforts to influence their culture precisely as Catholics opens the possibility to greater divisiveness and discord within society. Better, they may say, to have less religious influence rather than more. During his pilgrimage to the Shrine of Aparecida in Brazil, Pope Benedict offered an answer to that concern:

> Ultimately, it is only the truth that can bring unity, and the proof of this is love. That is why Christ, being in truth the incarnate *Logos*, "love to the end," is not alien to any culture, nor to any person; on the contrary, the response that he seeks in the heart of cultures is what gives them their ultimate identity, uniting humanity and at the same time respecting the wealth of diversity, opening people everywhere to growth in genuine humanity, in authentic progress.[19]

This book has attempted to outline some approaches that may prove especially fruitful in this regard. If I were to summarize them, I would say that ultimately the power of Catholics to transform America into a culture of life and a civilization of love will lie in the power of their example more than in the power of the ballot box, even though the ballot box is important. The early Christians did not take over the Roman Empire by electoral choice: there were no elections to speak of in those days. Rather they did so by their example, by holding out the possibility of a life that was higher, more beautiful, and above all more authentic than the vulgarity, violence, and greed of late antiquity. Christians today have the same opportunity to offer another way to a world that is also surfeited with these same problems.

Contemporary culture now offers us an astounding variety of lifestyles and ways of defining the "good life." It offers us as well an equally astounding number of ways of achieving whatever "good life" we may choose. Despite this (some might say precisely because of this), the words still echo toward us from the book of Genesis: speaking to Adam, God asks, "Where are you?" The Lord is still calling. Those who may hear these words, in turn make these words their own. They, too, ask, "Where is the man or

woman that the Lord has made?" Where is that person of whom
the saints said, "The glory of God is man fully alive"? Where is
the person created and redeemed by Christ? Where is the person
who joyfully lives the vocation to love to which humanity has
been called by Christ? Where can we find this "new" Adam in the
day-to-day world around us?

It is the responsibility of Christians to show the world this
new Adam.

They will do so by their actions, by their attitudes, and by their
influence. But above all, they will do so by their love. This love is
a matter not of mere high-minded sentimentality but of genuine
compassion tempered with a well-grounded realism. It is a love
that offers hope not only for eternity but for a better way of life
on this earth. It is a love that offers the promise of healing both
the spiritual and material ills of humanity. It is the love of which
Christ spoke when, after his resurrection, he asked Peter if he
loved him.[20]

Peter replied, "Yes, Lord; you know that I love you."

And to this Christ replied, "Feed my sheep."

SUGGESTIONS FOR CONTEMPLATION AND ACTION

1. Consider yourself as a representative of Christ in the
   world today. What do you do on a day-to-day basis to
   represent Christ? How do your actions and attitudes
   reflect his teachings? If you have never thought of this
   before, reflect on what you might do to bring Christ's
   teachings more out into the world.

2. Think about the interaction between your role as a
   religious believer and your role as a citizen. How do the
   values of one influence the other? Do you keep them in
   separate, watertight areas of your mind, or do they reflect
   and influence each other?

3. What do your political positions have to do with your faith? Do you vote your faith, or do you vote your pocketbook? Think about which political figures and positions you believe most truly represent Christ's teachings today, and think about how and whether you support them.

4. If you have children, ask yourself what you do to educate them in your faith. Does the education that they are receiving reflect your own values and beliefs? If not, consider how you might introduce more of your values into their education.

5. Spend some time reflecting on people you disagree with in terms of faith or politics. What sort of resentments or grievances are you harboring against them? Do these feelings bring you closer to the love of Christ or further from it? Think about ways in which you can forgive and love even those you disagree with.

6. What is your definition of love? What is your experience of love? How do you express the truth of love in your life?

Notes

EPIGRAPH

1. Benedict XVI (Joseph Ratzinger), *Message for World Youth Day* (2007).

INTRODUCTION

1. Huntington, *Who Are We?*, Part I, "The Issues of Identity," 1–34.
2. Churchill, 1689.
3. Kennedy.
4. Fukuyama.
5. Huntington, *Who Are We?*, 221.
6. Huntington, *Who Are We?*, 340.
7. Spiegelman, excerpted in Brunetti, 158.
8. Weaver.
9. Although Pope Paul VI first coined and used the phrase, for example, in his *Address at the Close of the Holy Year* (1975), it was Pope John Paul II who repeatedly used the phrase and developed it as a major subject throughout his pontificate. One of his earliest uses of the phrase is found in his second encyclical, *Dives in Misericordia*, §14 (1980)

CHAPTER 1: THE POWER OF CHRIST TO TRANSFORM CULTURE

1. John Paul II, *Redemptoris Missio*, §37.
2. Acts 17:22–33.
3. Brown, 309–11.
4. Thucydides, 2.41.

5. Cicero, *Pro Flacco*, 26:62.
6. Acts 17:21.
7. Acts 17:22.
8. Acts 17:28.
9. Acts 17:32.
10. Acts 17:29.
11. Pasternak, 10.
12. Acts 17:28.
13. Acts 17:27.
14. Huntington, *The Clash of Civilizations*, 57.
15. 1 John 4:8.
16. Huntington, *The Clash of Civilizations*, 214.
17. Locke.
18. Fisher and Rohter.
19. Macaulay, *History of England*, ch. 3; in Macaulay, 336.
20. Macaulay, 339.
21. Benedict XVI (Joseph Ratzinger), *Values in a Time of Upheaval*, 25.
22. Benedict XVI (Joseph Ratzinger), *Values in a Time of Upheaval*, 71.
23. Benedict XVI (Joseph Ratzinger), *Values in a Time of Upheaval*, 49.
24. Benedict XVI (Joseph Ratzinger), *Values in a Time of Upheaval*, 63.
25. St. Thomas Aquinas, Quest. 91, Art. 2, Reply Obj. 1; in Pegis, 618.
26. C. S. Lewis, 28–29.
27. Matthew 22:35–40.
28. Albom, 40.
29. Albom, 52.
30. John Paul II, *Familiaris Consortio*, §11.
31. Bernard Lewis.

CHAPTER 2: A CULTURE OF SUSPICION

1. Brinkley and Fenster, xiii.
2. Brinkley and Fenster, ix.
3. Nietzsche, *The Gay Science*, 279. See also 167, 181.
4. Nietzsche, *Human, All Too Human*, 79. Emphasis here and in subsequent quotations in this book from the original unless otherwise noted.
5. Nietzsche, *The Gay Science*, 187.

6. Nietzsche, *Thus Spoke Zarathustra*, 274.

7. Nietzsche, *Thus Spoke Zarathustra*, 12.

8. Freud, *Civilization and Its Discontents*, 10–11.

9. Freud, *Civilization and Its Discontents*, 13–15.

10. Freud, *Civilization and Its Discontents*, 22.

11. Marx, "Contribution to the Critique of Hegel's *Philosophy of Right*," Introduction.

12. Ricoeur, *Freud and Philosophy*, 33.

13. Freud, *Civilization and Its Discontents*, 66.

14. Ricoeur, *Freud and Philosophy*, 304.

15. Council of Vatican II, *Gaudium et Spes*, §22.

16. John Paul II, *Redemptor Hominis*, §10.

17. John Paul II, *Redemptor Hominis*, §8; cf. Council of Vatican II. *Gaudium et Spes*, 22. *Acta Apostolicae Sedis* 58 (1966): 1042–43.

18. John Paul II, *Redemptor Hominis*, §§12, 16.

19. John Paul II, *Redemptor Hominis*, §12.

20. John Paul II, *Redemptor Hominis*, §§8, 10.

21. John Paul II, *Redemptor Hominis*, §7.

22. John Paul II, *Redemptor Hominis*, §14.

23. 1 John 4:16.

24. Benedict XVI, *Deus Caritas Est*, §2.

25. See Nygren for a comprehensive treatment of this theme.

26. Benedict XVI, *Deus Caritas Est*, §3.

27. Benedict XVI, *Deus Caritas Est*, §4.

28. Benedict XVI, *Deus Caritas Est*, §6.

29. Benedict XVI, *Deus Caritas Est*, §7.

30. Benedict XVI, *Deus Caritas Est*, §7.

31. Ricoeur, *Freud and Philosophy*, 304.

CHAPTER 3: CRAFTSMEN OF A NEW HUMANITY

1. Mickiwewicz quoted in Rosen.

2. Gebhardt, quoted in Weigel, *Witness to Hope*, 39.

3. Dante, *Paradiso* 33.145. Divine Comedy, Volume 5, "Divine Comedy III. Part 1" Pg. 381.

4. Genesis 1:26.

5. Matthew 12.31.

6. John Paul II, *Memory and Identity*, 7.

7. Solovyov, 42.

8. Solovyov, 45.

9. von Balthasar, 143.

10. Council of Vatican II, *Gaudium et Spes*, §22.

11. John Paul II, *Redemptor Hominis*, §10.

12. John Paul II, *Redemptor Hominis*, §12.

13. Eliot, *Notes towards the Definition of Culture*, 32.

14. Mauriac, preface to Weigel, xviii.

15. Carl Becker, 31.

16. Merton, 126, 127.

17. Ambrose, 90, 197.

18. Berns, 68–69.

19. McGuffey, Lesson 1, 1–6.

20. Coles, *The Moral Intelligence of Children* and *The Moral Life of Children*.

21. Bryk, Lee, and Holland, 301.

22. John Paul II, "Message of His Holiness Pope John Paul II for the Celebration of the World Day of Peace, January 1, 2001."

CHAPTER 4: A DIGNITY THAT BRINGS DEMANDS

1. Bernard-Henri Lévy, 10.

2. Jahn.

3. Branch, 227.

4. Paul VI, "Address to the Last General Meeting of Vatican Council II," 63.

5. Paul VI, "Address to the Last General Meeting of Vatican Council II," 61.

6. John Paul II, *Christifideles Laici*, §17.

7. Council of Vatican II, *Lumen Gentium,* §31.

8. John Paul II, *Christifideles Laici*, §17.

9. Synod Fathers, *Propositio 4*, quoted in John Paul II, *Christifideles Laici*, §15.

10. John Paul II, *Laborem Exercens*, §9.

11. Benedict XVI, *Deus Caritas Est,* §30.

12. Hobbes, chap. 6.

13. See Luke 6:31.

14. See Luke 10:31–33.

15. Paul VI, "Address to the Last General Meeting of Vatican Council II," §63.

16. Benedict XVI, *Deus Caritas Est*, §34.

17. Lahood.

18. Teresa of Calcutta, "Nobel Prize Address Lecture."

19. Lahood.

20. Paul VI, quoted in John Paul II, *Christifideles Laici*, §19.

21. John Paul II, *Christifideles Laici*, §20.

22. Afflerback, 19–20.

23. Luke 16:19–26, NRSV.

24. Teresa of Calcutta, *Mother Teresa: Come Be My Light*.

25. Teresa of Calcutta, *Mother Teresa: Come Be My Light*, 173.

26. Luke 10:21.

27. Teresa of Calcutta, "Quotes from Mother Teresa."

28. Benedict XVI, *Deus Caritas Est*, §18.

29. Cameron, section on "The Human Drama."

30. Paul VI, *Address to the Last General Meeting of Vatican Council II*, 63.

31. Council of Vatican II, *Gaudium et Spes*, §24.

32. John Paul II, *Letter to Artists*, §§ 1–2.

33. John Paul II (Karol Wojtyla), *Radiation of Fatherhood*.

34. John Paul II (Karol Wojtyla), *Radiation of Fatherhood*, part 3, scene 2.

35. Benedict XVI, *Deus Caritas Est*, §31.

36. King, "I See the Promised Land," in *A Testament of Hope: The Essential Writings and Speeches of Martin Luther King, Jr.*, 285.

CHAPTER 5: THE DOMESTIC CHURCH

1. Genesis 1:27.

2. Quoted in Ouellet, 26.

3. Augustine, *The Trinity*, 20.

4. Augustine, *The Trinity* (14.3–4), 374–88.

5. Augustine, *The Trinity*. (14.3), 379.

6. John Paul II, *Letter to Families*, §6.

7. Scola, 27.

8. Ouellet, 111.

9. Ouellet, 111.

10. John Paul II, *Mulieris Dignitatem*, §7.
11. Ouellet, 114.
12. Browning, *Sonnets from the Portuguese*, 4; in *The Oxford Book of English Verse*, 815.
13. Ouellet, 115.
14. 1 Corinthians 13:4–8, NRSV.
15. Ouellet, 115.
16. John Paul II, *Familiaris Consortio*, §39. The translation of the title means "Family Partnership"; the English title of this document is *The Christian Family in the Modern World*.
17. Hughes.
18. Whitehead, 72.
19. Waite, et al., Executive Summary.
20. Marquardt, 188–89.
21. Lawton and Bures, 106.
22. St. Thomas Aquinas, *Summa Theologica*, Supplement to part III, q. 41.
23. John Paul II, *Familiaris Consortio*, §20.
24. Quoted in Ouellet, 43.
25. John Paul II, *Letter to Families*, §14.
26. Paul VI, *Humanae Vitae*, §17.
27. John Paul II, *Theology of the Body*, 398.
28. John Paul II, *Letter to Families*, §12.
29. Shivanandan, 251.
30. Oddens, 277–86.
31. Doyle.
32. Fehring, 179–87. See also Fehring and Donna M. Lawrence, "Spiritual Well-Being, Self-Esteem and Intimacy among Couples Using Natural Family Planning," *Linacre Quarterly* 61, no. 3 (1994): 18–29.
33. John Paul II, *Letter to Families*, §15.
34. Joshua 24:15.
35. Ephesians 5:25.
36. John Chrysostom, *Homilies on Genesis*, 6.2; quoted in Ouellet, 41.
37. John Paul II, Discourse at the Third General Assembly of the Latin American Bishops, §4; in *Acta Apostolicae Sedis* 71 (1979): 204; quoted in Ouellet, 3.

38. John Paul II, *Familiaris Consortio*, §17.

39. Scola, 211.

40. Scola, 211.

41. Tertullian, Ad Uxorem, 2:8, 6–8: CCL 1: 393. Quoted in John Paul II, *Familiaris Consortio*, §13.

CHAPTER 6: GLOBALIZATION AND THE GOSPEL OF WORK

1. Szulc, 118.

2. Weigel, 57.

3. John Paul II, *Gift and Mystery*, 20–22.

4. Kwitny, 44.

5. Its English title is *The Condition of Labor*, or *On the Condition of Workers*.

6. Acts 4:32.

7. Joseph N. Moody, "Leo XIII and the Social Crisis," in Gargan, 68–69.

8. Quoted in Moody, 75.

9. Marx and Engels.

10. Leo XIII, §3.

11. Leo XIII, §6.

12. Leo XIII, §8.

13. Leo XIII, §17.

14. Leo XIII, §20.

15. Tsu, §38.

16. Leo XIII, §25.

17. Augustine, "Homily 7 on the First Epistle of John," §8.

18. Leo XIII, §49.

19. Leo XIII, §37.

20. Leo XIII, §42.

21. Pius XI, §22.

22. Mills, 63–64.

23. Robinson.

24. Hochschild, 198.

25. Hochschild, 147.

26. Leo XIII, §41.

27. John Paul II, *Centesimus Annus*, §11.

28. Genesis 1:28.

29. John Paul II, *Laborem Exercens*, §6.
30. Genesis 2:15.
31. John Paul II, *Laborem Exercens*, §6.
32. John Paul II, *Laborem Exercens*, §14.
33. de Botton, 100.
34. John Paul II, *Centesimus Annus*, §19.
35. John Paul II, *Centesimus Annus*, §35.
36. Terkel, 167.
37. Bornstein, 49.
38. Paul VI, *Populorum Progressio*, §59.
39. John Paul II, *Centesimus Annus*, §58.
40. Gary Becker.
41. Friedman, 354.
42. Zedillo.
43. Paul VI, *Populorum Progressio*, §40.
44. Paul VI, *Populorum Progressio*, §20.
45. Friedman, 4.
46. Friedman, 16.
47. Friedman, 300.
48. Paul VI, *Populorum Progressio*, §17.
49. Bornstein, 3.
50. Benedict XVI, Inaugural Session of the Fifth General Conference of the Bishops of Latin America and the Caribbean, §2.

CHAPTER 7: ETHICS IN THE MARKETPLACE

1. Havel, 4.
2. *The Corporation,* synopsis.
3. CBS Evening News, "Enron Traders Caught on Tape."
4. Alcaly, 179.
5. Rosenberg, 46.
6. Drucker, 63–64.
7. Collins and Porras, 8.
8. Rossbacher.
9. Boudreau, 32–39.
10. Brinkley and Fenster, 110.
11. Brinkley and Fenster, 109.

12. Brinkley and Fenster, 122–23.

13. John Paul II, *Laborem Exercens*, §6.

14. Bogle, 221–22.

15. Novak.

16. John Paul II, *Centesimus Annus*, §38.

CHAPTER 8: A PEOPLE OF LIFE AND FOR LIFE

1. The following account relies on the biography page "St. Maximilian Kolbe" at http://www.catholic-pages.com/saints/st_maximilian.asp.

2. Romans 12:21.

3. John Paul II, *Memory and Identity*, 21.

4. John Paul II, *Evangelium Vitae*, §95. The English title of this encyclical is *On the Value and Inviolability of Human Life*.

5. *Roe v. Wade*, 410 U.S. 113 (1973).

6. *Byrn v. New York City Health & Hospital Corporation*, 31 N.Y.2d 194; 286 N.E.2d 887 (1972).

7. *Plessy v. Ferguson*, 163 U.S. 537 (1896) at 551.

8. Alexander, 39–40.

9. "Hippocratic Oath." For newer versions of the oath, see St. Louis University, School of Medicine "The Hippocratic Oath" http://medschool.slu.edu/studentaffairs/index.phtml?page=hippocratic oath and PBS "The Hippocratic Oath—Modern Version," www.pbs.org/wgbh/nova/doctors/oath_modern.html.

10. Wolf, 33.

11. John Paul II, *Evangelium Vitae*, §§18–20.

12. John Paul II, *Evangelium Vitae*, §18.

13. John Paul II, *Evangelium Vitae*, §18. John Paul II's acknowledgment in §18 of the suffering and sense of hopelessness that often pervades these decisions against life, as well as his sensitivity shown in §99 in discussing pastoral responses to women who have had abortions, reflect the depth of commitment to "solidarity" that runs through *Evangelium Vitae*.

14. John Paul II, *Evangelium Vitae*, §§18–19.

15. John Paul II, *Evangelium Vitae*, §18.

16. John Paul II, *Evangelium Vitae*, §§19–20.

17. England. "The Act of Supremacy," 1534.
18. Miller, in More, 14:2, 775.
19. More, *De Tristitia Christi*, in More, 14:1, 3–4.
20. Teresa of Calcutta, "Nobel Peace Prize Lecture."
21. John Paul II, *Evangelium Vitae*, §6.
22. John Paul II, *Evangelium Vitae*, §2.

CHAPTER 9: A CONTINENT OF BAPTIZED CHRISTIANS
1. Matthew 6:21.
2. Mark 10:21.
3. Matthew 25:37–45.
4. John Paul II, "Message of the Holy Father for the World Migration Day, 2000," §5.
5. Jenkins, *The Next Christendom*, 215–16.
6. Jenkins, *The Next Christendom*, 195.
7. Jenkins, *The Next Christendom*, 83–84.
8. Benedict XVI, *Deus Charitas Est*, §25.
9. John Paul II, *Ecclesia in America*, §5.
10. Synod of Bishops, §25; boldface is in the original document.
11. Benedict XVI (Joseph Ratzinger), *What It Means to Be a Christian*, 69.
12. Synod of Bishops, §66.
13. United States Conference of Catholic Bishops.
14. Synod of Bishops, §19.
15. Synod of Bishops, §4.
16. Benedict XVI, Inaugural Session of the Fifth General Conference of the Bishops of Latin America and the Caribbean, §1.
17. Pastor.
18. Pastor.
19. Jenkins, *The Next Christendom*, 92.
20. Jenkins, *The Next Christendom*, 94.
21. Jenkins, *The Next Christendom*, 95.
22. John Paul II, *Ecclesia in America*, §11.
23. Liddycoat, "Hope Springs from Wells."
24. John Paul II, *Letter to Families*, §15.

CONCLUSION

1. John Paul II, *The Pope Speaks to the American Church*, 115–116.
2. John Paul II, *The Pope Speaks to the American Church*, 116.
3. John Paul II, *The Pope Speaks to the American Church*, 113.
4. Benedict XVI (Joseph Ratzinger), *Introduction to Christianity*, 39.
5. Benedict XVI (Joseph Ratzinger), *Introduction to Christianity*, 43.
6. Benedict XVI, *Deus Caritas Est*, 31(b).
7. John 18:36.
8. John 17:16.
9. John 17:18.
10. Quoted in Niebuhr, 75.
11. For an online version of this text, see http://www.angelfire.com/co/JeffersonBible/.
12. James, 83.
13. Johnson, 149.
14. Niebuhr, 19.
15. John Paul II, *Evangelium Vitae*, §29.
16. Benedict XVI, *Deus Caritas Est*, §31.
17. Eliot, *The Idea of a Christian Society*, 4.
18. Benedict XVI, *Christianity and the Crisis of Cultures*, 52.
19. Benedict XVI, Inaugural Session of the Fifth General Conference of the Bishops of Latin America and the Caribbean, §1.
20. John 21:17.

Selected Bibliography

Afflerback, Fred. "Praying with Prisoners." From "Faith in Action." *Columbia Magazine,* August 2007, 19–20.

Albom, Mitch. *Tuesdays with Morrie: An Old Man, A Young Man, and Life's Greatest Lesson.* New York: Doubleday, 1997.

Alcaly, Roger. *The New Economy: And What It Means for America's Future.* New York: Farrar, Straus & Giroux, 2003.

Alexander, Leo. "Medical Science under Dictatorship." *New England Journal of Medicine* 241.2 (14 July 1949): 39–47.

Alighieri, Dante. *The Divine Comedy.* Translated with a commentary by Charles S. Singleton. 6 vols. Princeton: Princeton/Bollingen, 1970–1975.

Ambrose, Stephen. *To America: Personal Reflections of an Historian.* New York: Simon & Schuster, 2002.

Anderson, Carl A. "The New Areopagus of Culture, Conscience and Human Dignity." *Anthropotes* 8:200 (1992).

Applebaum, Anne. *Gulag: A History.* New York: Doubleday, 2003.

Augustine of Hippo. *Confessions.* Translated by R. S. Pine-Coffin. New York: Dorset, 1986.

———. "Homily 7 on the First Epistle of John." In *St. Augustine: Ten Homilies on the First Epistle of John.* Translated by Rev. H. Browne and edited by Philip Schaff. New York: Christian Literature Publishing, 1886, 501–5. http://www.ccel.org/ccel/schaff/npnf107 .iv.x.html.

————. *The Trinity.* Translated by Edmund Hill, O.P. Brooklyn, NY: New City Press, 1991.

Becker, Carl. *The Heavenly City of the Eighteenth-Century Philosophers.* New Haven: Yale Univ. Press, 1932.

Becker, Gary S. "How Globalization Helps the Poor." *Business Week,* April 21, 2003.

Benedict XVI. (Joseph Ratzinger) *Christianity and the Crisis of Cultures.* San Francisco: Ignatius Press, 2006.

————. (Joseph Ratzinger) *Church, Ecumenism and Politics: New Essays in Ecclesiology.* New York: St. Paul Publications, 1988.

————. *Deus Caritas Est.* Vatican City: Libreria Editrice Vaticana, 2005. http://www.vatican.va/holy_father/benedict_xvi/encyclicals/documents/hf_ben-xvi_enc_20051225_deus-caritas-est_en.html.

————. Inaugural Session of the Fifth General Conference of the Bishops of Latin America and the Caribbean. May 13, 2007. Libreria Editrice Vaticana. http://www.vatican.va/holy_father/benedict_xvi/speeches/2007/may/documents/hf_ben-xvi_spe_20070513_conference-aparecida_en.html.

————. (Joseph Ratzinger) *Introduction to Christianity.* Translated by J. R. Foster. San Francisco: Ignatius Press, 1990.

————. (Joseph Ratzinger) *Values in a Time of Upheaval.* Translated by Brian McNeil. San Francisco: Ignatius Press, 2006.

————. (Joseph Ratzinger) *What It Means to Be a Christian.* Translated by Henry Taylor. San Francisco: Ignatius Press, 2006.

————. (Joseph Ratzinger) *Salt of the Earth: Christianity and the Catholic Church at the End of the Millennium.* Interview with Peter Seewald; translated by Adrian Walker. San Francisco: Ignatius Press, 1997.

————. *Spe Salvi.* Vatican City: Libreria Editrice Vaticana, 2007. http://www.vatican.va/holy_father/benedict_xvi/encyclicals/documents/hf_ben-xvi_enc_20071130_spe-salvi_en.html.

————. *The Essential Pope Benedict XVI: His central writings and speeches.* Edited by John F. Thornton and Susan B. Varenne; introduction by D. Vincent Twomey. New York: HarperSanFrancisco, 2007.

———. (Joseph Ratzinger) Benedict XVI, and Jurgen Habermas. *Dialectics of Secularization: On Reason and Religion.* San Francisco: Ignatius Press, 2007.

Berns, Walter. *Making Patriots.* Chicago: Univ. of Chicago Press, 2001.

Bertens, Hans. *The Idea of the Postmodern: A History.* New York: Routledge, 1995.

Bockris, John O'M. *The New Paradigm: A Confrontation between Physics and the Paranormal Phenomena.* College Station, TX: D & M Publishing, 2004.

Bogle, John C. *The Battle for the Soul of Capitalism.* New Haven: Yale Univ. Press, 2005.

Bonhoeffer, Dietrich. *Christ the Center.* New York: HarperCollins, 1978.

———. *Who Is Christ for Us?* Edited by Craig Nessan and Renate Wind. Philadelphia: Fortress, 2002.

Bornstein, David. *How to Change the World: Social Entrepreneurs and the Power of New Ideas.* Oxford: Oxford Univ. Press, 2004.

Boudreau, Dale. "Sources of the Fraternal Spirit." *Gnosis* 44 (Summer 1997): 32–39.

Branch, Taylor. *Parting the Waters: America in the King Years, 1954–63.* New York: Simon & Schuster, 1989.

Brinkley, Douglas, and Julie M. Fenster. *Parish Priest: Father Michael McGivney and American Catholicism.* New York: William Morrow, 2006.

Brown, Raymond E. *An Introduction to the New Testament.* New York: Doubleday, 1996.

Browning, Elizabeth Barrett. "Sonnets from the Portuguese, 4." In *The Oxford Book of English Verse,* edited by Arthur Quiller-Couch. Oxford: Clarendon Press: 1939, 815.

Brunetti, Ivan, ed. *An Anthology of Graphic Fiction, Cartoons, and True Stories.* New Haven: Yale Univ. Press, 2006.

Bryk, Anthony S., Valerie E. Lee, and Peter B. Holland. *Catholic Schools and the Common Good.* Cambridge: Harvard Univ. Press, 1993.

Buber, Martin. *I and Thou.* Translated by Ronald Gregor Smith 2nd ed. Edinburgh: T & T Clark, 1958.

Byrn v. New York City Health & Hospitals Corp. 31 N.Y.2d 194, 286 N. E.2d 887, 335 N.Y.S.2d 390 (1972), appeal dismissed, 410 U.S. 949 (1973).

Cameron, Peter. "The Role of Theatre in the Evangelization of Culture." Lecture given at the Institute for the Psychological Sciences. The Cosmos Club, Washington, D.C. January 23, 2004. Black Friars Theater Web site. http://www.blackfriars rep.com/productions/evangelizationtheater.htm.

CBS Evening News. "Enron Traders Caught on Tape." June 1, 2004. http://www.cbsnews.com/stories/2004/06/01/evening news/main620626.shtml.

Churchill, Winston. "The Ever-Widening War." In *The Churchill War Papers*. Vol. 3. Compiled and edited by Martin Gilbert. New York: W. W. Norton, 1993.

Cicero, M. Tullius. *The Orations of Marcus Tullius Cicero*. Translated by C. D. Yonge. London: Henry G. Bohn, 1856. Perseus Digital Library. http://www.perseus.tufts.edu/cgi-bin/ptext?lookup=Cic.+Flac.+1.

Coles, Robert. *The Moral Intelligence of Children: How to Raise a Moral Child*. New York: Penguin, 1998.

———. *The Moral Life of Children*. New York: Penguin, 1993.

Collins, James, and Jerry Porras. *Built to Last: Successful Habits of Visionary Companies*. New York: HarperCollins, 1994.

Commager, Henry Steele, and Milton Cantor, eds. *Documents of American History*. 2 vols. Englewood Cliffs, NJ: Prentice Hall, 1988.

Corporation, The. Directed by Mark Achbar and Jennifer Abbott. Written by Joel Bakan. Big Picture Media Corporation, 2004. http://www.thecorporation.com/index.php?page_id=2.

Council of Vatican II. *Gaudium et Spes*. Promulgated by Pope Paul VI, December 7, 1965. Vatican City: Libreria Editrice Vaticana. http://www.vatican.va/archive/hist_councils/ii_vatican_council/ documents/vat-ii_cons_19651207_gaudium-et-spes_en.html.

———. Council of Vatican II. *Lumen Gentium*. Promulgated by Pope Paul VI, November 21, 1964. Vatican City: Libreria Editrice

Vaticana. http://www.vatican.va/archive/hist_councils/ii_vatican_council/documents/vat-ii_const_19641121_lumen-gentium_en.html.

Dawson, Christopher. *Religion and the Modern State*. New York: Sheed & Ward, 1938.

de Botton, Alain. *Status Anxiety*. New York: Vintage, 2004.

Doyle, Fletcher. *Natural Family Planning Blessed Our Marriage*. Cincinnati: Servant Publications, 2006.

Drucker, Peter F. *The Essential Drucker*. New York: Collins Business, 2001.

Dulles, Avery. *The Splendor of Faith: The Theological Vision of Pope John Paul II*. New York: Crossroad, 2003.

Eliot, T. S. *The Idea of a Christian Society*. New York: Harcourt, Brace & World, 1940.

———. *Notes towards the Definition of Culture*. New York: Harcourt, Brace, 1949.

England. Parliament of England under Henry VIII. "The Act of Supremacy"; Luminarium: Encyclopedia Project. "The Act of Supremacy, 1534." http://www.luminarium.org/encyclopedia/act supremacy.htm.

Fehring, Richard J. "Reflections on the Spirituality of Natural Family Planning." *Chicago Studies* 33, no. 2 (1994): 179–87.

Fehring, Richard, and Donna M. Lawrence. "Spiritual Well-Being, Self-Esteem and Intimacy among Couples Using Natural Family Planning." *Linacre Quarterly* 61, no. 3, (1994): 18–29.

Fisher, Ian, and Larry Rohter. "The Pope Denounces Capitalism and Marxism." *New York Times,* May 14 2007. http://www.nytimes.com/2007/05/14/world/americas/14pope.html?_r=1&oref=slogin.

Freud, Sigmund. *Civilization and Its Discontents*. Translated and edited by James Strachey. Biographical introduction by Peter Gay. New York: W. W. Norton, 1989

Friedman, Benjamin M. *The Moral Consequences of Economic Growth*. New York: Knopf, 2005.

Fukuyama, Francis. *The End of History and the Last Man.* New York: Free Press, 1992.

Gargan, Edward T., ed. *Leo XIII and the Modern World.* New York: Sheed & Ward, 1961.

George, Robert. *The Clash of Orthodoxies: Law, Religion, and Morality in Crisis.* Wilmington, DE.: ISI Books, 2001.

——.George, Robert and Jean Bethke Elshtain. *The Meaning of Marriage: Family, State, Market, and Morals.*

Gladwell, Malcolm. *The Tipping Point: How Little Things Can Make a Big Difference.* Boston: Little, Brown, 2000.

Grene, David, and Richmond Lattimore, eds. *The Complete Greek Tragedies.* 4 vols. Chicago: Univ. of Chicago Press, 1959.

Guardini, Romano. *The End of the Modern World.* Chicago: Regnery, 1968.

Guénon, René. *The Reign of Quantity and the Signs of the Times.* Translated by Lord Northbourne. Baltimore: Penguin, 1972.

Hamilton, Alexander, John Jay, and James Madison. *The Federalist Papers.* New York: Mentor, 1999.

Havel, Vaclav. *The Art of the Impossible: Politics as Morality in Practice.* New York: Fromm International, 1998.

——. *Living in Truth.* London: Faber and Faber, 1986.

"Hippocratic Oath." Translated by Ludwig Edelstein. From *The Hippocratic Oath: Text, Translation, and Interpretation.* Baltimore: Johns Hopkins Press, 1943. Nova Online. http://www.pbs.org/wgbh/nova/doctors/oath_classical.html.

Hobbes, Thomas. *Leviathan: With Selected Variants from the Latin Edition of 1668.* Edited by Edwin Curley. Indianapolis: Hackett, 1994.

Hochschild, Arlie Russell. *The Commercialization of Intimate Life: Notes from Home and Work.* Berkeley: Univ. of California Press, 2003.

The Holy Bible. Revised Standard Version, Catholic Edition. Oxford: Oxford Univ. Press, 2004.

Hughes, Robert. "The Demographics of Divorce—United States and Missouri." Missouri Families. http://missourifamilies.org/FEATURES/divorcearticles/divorcefeature17.htm.

Huntington, Samuel P. *The Clash of Civilizations and the Remaking of World Order.* New York: Simon & Schuster, 1996.

———. *Who Are We? The Challenges to America's National Identity.* New York: Simon & Schuster, 2004.

Jahn, Gunnar. "Presentation Speech." Nobel Peace Prize 1964. http://nobelprize.org/nobel_prizes/peace/laureates/1964/press .html.

James, William. *The Varieties of Religious Experience.* London: Longmans, Green, 1910.

Jefferson, Thomas. *Jefferson Bible: The Life and Morals of Jesus of Nazareth Extracted Textually from the Gospels.* New York: Holt, 1995. Version edited by Eyler Robert Coates at http://www.angelfire. com/co/JeffersonBible/.

Jenkins, Philip. *The New Anti-Catholicism: The Last Acceptable Prejudice.* New York: Oxford Univ. Press, 2003.

———. *The New Faces of Christianity: Believing the Bible in the Global South.* New York: Oxford Univ. Press, 2006.

———. *The Next Christendom: The Coming of Global Christianity.* New York: Oxford Univ. Press, 2002.

John Paul II. *Centesimus Annus.* Vatican City: Libreria Editrice Vaticana, 1991. http://www.vatican.va/holy_father/john_paul_ ii/encyclicals/documents/hf_jp-ii_enc_01051991_centesimus -annus_en.html.

———. *Christifideles Laici.* Vatican City: Libreria Editrice Vaticana, 1988. http://www.vatican.va/holy_father/john_paul_ii/apost_ exhortations/documents/hf_jp-ii_exh_30121988_christifi- deles-laici_en.html.

———. *Crossing the Threshold of Hope.* Edited by Vittorio Messori; Translated by Jenny McPhee and Martha McPhee. New York: Knopf, 1994.

———. *Ecclesia in America.* Vatican City: Libreria Editrice Vaticana, 1999. http://www.vatican.va/holy_father/john_paul_ii/apost_ exhortations/documents/hf_jp-ii_exh_22011999_ecclesia- in-america_en.html.

———. *Evangelium Vitae: Enciclica e Commenti*. Vatican City: Libreria Editrice Vaticana, 1995. http://www.vatican.va/holy_father/ john_paul_ii/encyclicals/documents/hf_jp-ii_enc_25031995_ evangelium-vitae_en.html.

———. *Familiaris Consortio*. Vatican City: Libreria Editrice Vaticana, 1981. http://www.vatican.va/holy_father/john_paul_ii/apost_ exhortations/documents/hf_jp-ii_exh_19811122_familiaris-consortio_en.html.

———. *Gift and Mystery*. New York: Doubleday, 1996.

———. *Laborem Exercens*. Vatican City: Libreria Editrice Vaticana, 1981. http://www.vatican.va/holy_father/john_paul_ii/encyc-licals/documents/hf_jp-ii_enc_14091981_laborem-exercens_ en.html.

———. *Letter of His Holiness Pope John Paul II to Artists*. Vatican City: Libreria Editrice Vaticana, 1999. http://www.vatican.va/holy_ father/john_paul_ii/letters/documents/hf_jp-ii_let_23041999_ artists_en.html.

———. *Letter to Families*. Vatican City: Libreria Editrice Vaticana, 1994. http://www.vatican.va/holy_father/john_paul_ii/letters/ documents/hf_jp-ii_let_02021994_families_en.html.

———. *Love and Responsibility*. New York: Farrar Straus & Giroux, 1981.

———. "Man Becomes the Image of God by Communion of Per-sons." General Audience, November 14, 1979. *L'Osservatore Romano,* November 19, 1979, 1. Eternal Word Television Net-work. http://www.ewtn.com/library/PAPALDOC/jp2tb9.htm.

———. "Meaning of Man's Original Solitude." General Audience, October 10, 1979. *L'Osservatore Romano,* October 15, 1979, 14. Eternal Word Television Network. http://www.ewtn.com/li-brary/PAPALDOC/jp2tb5.htm.

———. *Memory and Identity: Conversations at the Dawn of a Millennium*. New York: Rizzoli, 2005.

———. *Message of His Holiness Pope John Paul II for the Celebration of the World Day of Peace*. From the Vatican, January 1, 2001. http://www.vatican.

va/holy_father/john_paul_ii/messages/peace/documents/hf_
jp-ii_mes_20001208_xxxiv-world-day-for-peace_en.html.

———. *"Message of the Holy Father for the World Migration Day, 2000."*
From the Vatican, November 21, 1999. http://www.vatican.va/
holy_father/john_paul_ii/messages/migration/documents/hf_
jp-ii_mes_21111999_world-migration-day–2000_en.html.

———. *Mulieris Dignitatem.* Vatican City: Libreria Editrice Vaticana,
1988. http://www.vatican.va/holy_father/john_paul_ii/apost_let-
ters/documents/hf_jp-ii_apl_15081988_mulieris-dignitatem_
en.html.

———. (Karol Wojtyla) *Radiation of Fatherhood.* 1964. Love & Responsibility Foundation Web site. http://www.catholicculture.
com/Radiation_of_Fatherhood.pdf.

———. *Redemptor Hominis.* Vatican City: Libreria Editrice Vaticana,
1979. http://www.vatican.va/holy_father/john_paul_ii/encycli-
cals/documents/hf_jp-ii_enc_04031979_redemptor-hominis_
en.html.

———. *The Pope Speaks to the American Church.* New York: HarperSan-
Francisco, 1992.

———. *The Theology of the Body: Human Love in the Divine Plan.* Boston:
Pauline Books & Media, 1997.

Johnson, Paul. *A History of Christianity.* New York: Atheneum, 1987.

Kauffman, Christopher J. *Faith and Fraternalism: The History of the
Knights of Columbus.* Rev. ed. New York: Simon & Schuster, 1992.

———. *Patriotism and Fraternalism in the Knights of Columbus: A History of
the Fourth Degree.* New York: Herder & Herder, 2001.

Kennedy, John F. "Inaugural Address." Presidential Inauguration,
Washington, D.C. January 20, 1961. Avalon Project of Yale
Law School. http://www.yale.edu/lawweb/avalon/presiden/inaug/
kennedy.htm.

King, Martin Luther, Jr. *A Testament of Hope: The Essential Writings of
Martin Luther King, Jr.* Edited by James Washington. San Francisco: Harper & Row, 1986.

Kitto, H.D.F. *The Greeks.* London: Penguin, 1991.

Kwitny, Jonathan. *Man of the Century: The Life and Times of Pope John Paul II*. New York: Henry Holt, 1997.

Lahood, Dan. Interview by John Lander. From *Vocation of the Laity*. DVD. Produced by John Lander. Knights of Columbus. 2007.

Lasagna, Louis. "Hippocratic Oath." 1964. Nova Online. http://www.pbs.org/wgbh/nova/doctors/oath_modern.html.

Lawton, Leora, and Regina Bures. "Parental Divorce and the 'Switching' of Religious Identity." *Journal for the Scientific Study of Religion* 40, no. 1 (2001): 99–111.

Leo XIII. *Rerum Novarum*. Vatican City: Libreria Editrice Vaticana, 1891. http://www.vatican.va/holy_father/leo_xiii/encyclicals/documents/hf_l-xiii_enc_15051891_rerum-novarum_en.html.

Lévy, Bernard-Henri. *Sartre: The Philosopher of the Twentieth Century*. Cambridge, UK: Polity Press, 2003.

Lewis, Bernard. "The 2007 Irving Kristol Lecture." AEI Annual Dinner, Washington. http://www.aei.org/include/pub_print.asp?pubID=25815.

Lewis, C. S. *The Abolition of Man*. San Francisco: HarperSanFrancisco, 2001.

Liddycoat, Bob. "Hope Springs from Wells: Ted van der Zalm is bringing water to third world countries, a few copper coins at a time." *Thorold News,* July 19, 2003. http://www.warehouseofhope.com/tedstory.htm.

Locke, John. "A Letter Concerning Toleration." Translated by William Popple. Constitution Society Web site. http://www.constitution.org/jl/tolerati.htm.

Lubac, Henri de. *The Drama of Atheist Humanism*. San Francisco: Ignatius Press, 1995.

Lyotard, Jean-François. *The Postmodern Explained: Correspondence 1982–1985*. Minneapolis: Univ. of Minnesota Press, 1992.

Macaulay, Thomas Babington. *Selected Writings*. Edited by John Clive. Chicago: Univ. of Chicago Press, 1972.

Maritain, Jacques. *Christianity and Democracy*. San Francisco: Ignatius Press, 1986 [1943].

Marquardt, Elizabeth. *Between Two Worlds: The Inner Lives of Children of Divorce.* New York: Crown, 2005.

Marx, Karl. "Contribution to the Critique of Hegel's *Philosophy of Right.*" *Deutsch-Französische Jahrbücher*, February, 1844. Marxist Internet Archive. http://www.marxists.org/archive/marx/works/1843/critique-hpr/intro.htm.

Marx, Karl, and Friedrich Engels. *The Communist Manifesto.* Introduction by Martin Malia. New York: Penguin. http://www.anu.edu.au/polsci/marx/classics/manifesto.html.

Massa, Mark S. *Anti-Catholicism in America: The Last Acceptable Prejudice.* New York: Crossroads, 2003.

McGreevy, John T. *Catholicism and American Freedom.* New York: W. W. Norton, 2003.

McGuffey, William. *The Eclectic Fourth Reader.* Cincinnati: Truman and Smith, 1939. http://www.mcguffeyreaders.com/1836_original.htm.

Meacham, Jon. *American Gospel: God, the Founding Fathers and the Making of a Nation.* New York: Random House, 2006.

Melina, Livio, and Carl A. Anderson, eds. *The Way of Love: Reflections on Pope Benedict XVI's Encyclical* Deus Caritas Est. San Francisco: Ignatius Press, 2006.

Merton, Thomas. *The Seven Storey Mountain.* New York: Harcourt, Brace, 1948.

Mills, C. Wright. *White Collar: The American Middle Classes.* New York: Oxford Univ. Press, 1951.

Moody, Joseph N. "Leo XIII and the Social Crisis," in Gargan, *Leo XIII and the Modern World.* New York: Sheed & Ward, 1961. Pages 65–88.

Moore, Lorrie. *Self-Help: Stories.* Reprint, New York: Vintage, 2007.

More, St. Thomas. *The Complete Works of St. Thomas More.* 14 vols. Edited by Clarence Miller. New Haven: Yale Univ. Press, 1963–1997.

Mother Angelica. *Mother Angelica's Answers, Not Promises.* 2nd Edition. San Francisco: Ignatius Press, 1996.

Muggeridge, Malcolm. *Something Beautiful for God: Mother Teresa of Calcutta*. New York: Harper & Row, 1971.

Nichols, Aidan. *The Thought of Benedict XVI: An Introduction to the Theology of Joseph Ratzinger*. New York: Burns & Oates, 2005.

Neuhaus, Richard John. *America against Itself: Moral Vision and the Public Order*. Notre Dame: University of Notre Dame Press, 1992.

——. *Naked Public Square: Religion and Democracy in America*. Grand Rapids, MI: W.B. Eerdmans, 1986, 1984.

Niebuhr, H. Richard. *Christ and Culture*. New York: HarperCollins, 2001.

Nietzsche, Friedrich. *The Gay Science*. Translated by Walter Kaufman. New York: Vintage, 1974.

——. *Human, All Too Human: A Book for Free Spirits*. Translated by Marion Faber and Stephen Lehmann. Lincoln: Univ. of Nebraska Press, 1984.

——. *Thus Spoke Zarathustra*. Translated by Walter Kaufmann. New York: Vintage, 1966.

Noonan, Peggy. *A Heart, a Cross, and a Flag: America Today*. New York: Free Press, 2003.

——. *John Paul the Great: Remembering a Spiritual Father*. New York: Viking, 2005.

Novak, Michael. *Business as a Calling: Work and the Examined Life*. New York: Free Press, 1996.

Nygren, Anders. *Agape and Eros*. Translated by Philip Watson. 3 vols. London: SPCK, 1938.

Oddens, Björn J. "Women's Satisfaction with Birth Control: A Population Survey of Physical and Psychological Effects of Oral Contraceptives, Intrauterine Devices, Condoms, Natural Family Planning, and Sterilization among 1466 Women." *Contraception* 59 (1999): 277–86.

Orwell, George. *A Collection of Essays*. New York: Harcourt, Brace, Jovanovich, 1953.

Ouellet, Marc. *Divine Likeness: Toward a Trinitarian Anthropology of the Family*. Grand Rapids, MI: Eerdmans, 2006.

Oxford Book of English Verse: 1250–1918. Edited by Sir Arthur Quiller-Couch. Oxford: Oxford at the Clarendon Press, n.d.

Pasternak, Boris. *Doctor Zhivago.* Translated by Max Hayward and Manya Harari. New York: Pantheon, 1958.

Pastor, Robert A. "Breaking Out of the Box." *Newsweek*, March 27, 2006. http://www.msnbc.msn.com/id/11904430/site/newsweek/.

Paul VI. "Address to the Last General Meeting of Vatican Council II." *Documents of Vatican II.* Edited by Thurston Davis, S.J. New York: America Press, 1966, 57–64.

———. *Humanae Vitae.* Vatican City: Libreria Editrice Vaticana, 1968. http://www.vatican.va/holy_father/paul_vi/encyclicals/documents/hf_p-vi_enc_25071968_humanae-vitae_en.html.

———. *Populorum Progressio.* Vatican City: Libreria Editrice Vaticana, 1967. http://www.vatican.va/holy_father/paul_vi/encyclicals/documents/hf_p-vi_enc_26031967_populorum_en.html.

Pegis, Anton C., ed. *Introduction to St. Thomas Aquinas.* New York: Modern Library, 1948.

Pius XI. *Quadragesimo Anno.* Vatican City: Libreria Editrice Vaticana, 1931. http://www.vatican.va/holy_father/pius_xi/encyclicals/documents/hf_p-xi_enc_19310515_quadragesimo-anno_en.html.

Plato. *The Collected Dialogues.* Edited by Edith Hamilton and Huntington Cairns. Princeton: Princeton/Bollingen, 1963.

Plessy v. Ferguson. 163 U.S. 537 (1896) at 551.

Pound, Ezra. *The Cantos of Ezra Pound.* New York: New Directions, 1970.

Revel, Jean Francois. *Without Marx or Jesus: the New American Revolution Has Begun.* Afterword by Mary McCarthy. Translated by J. F. Bernard. Garden City, N.Y.: Doubleday, 1971.

Ricoeur, Paul. *Fallible Man.* Translated by Charles A. Kelbley. Rev. ed. New York: Fordham Univ. Press, 1986.

———. *Freud and Philosophy: An Essay on Interpretation.* New Haven: Yale Univ. Press, 1970.

Robinson, Joe. "Bring Back the 40-Hour Workweek—and Let Us Take a Long Vacation." *Los Angeles Times*, January 1, 2006. http://www.latimes.com/news/opinion/commentary/la-op-robinson 1jan01,0,7251877.story?coll=la-news-comment-opinions.

Roe v. Wade. 410 U.S. 113 (1973).

Rosen, David. Inaugural Fred and Lesley Israel Lecture. "Christian-Jewish Relations: The Legacy of Pope John Paul II." Program of Jewish Civilization. Georgetown Univ., Washington, D.C. February 2, 2004. http://www.ajc.org/site/apps/nl/content 3.asp?c=ijITI2PHKoG&b=846561&ct=1084013.

Rosenberg, John S. "An Education in Ethics." *Harvard Magazine* 109, no. 1 (2006). http://harvardmagazine.com/2006/09/an-education-in-ethics.html.

Rossbacher, Lisa. "Banking on Earthquakes." *Geotimes,* July 2005. http://www.geotimes.org/july05/column.html.

Rubenstein, Richard. *Aristotle's Children: How Christians, Muslims, and Jews Rediscovered Ancient Wisdom and Illuminated the Dark Ages.* New York: Harcourt, 2003.

Rutler, George William. *Beyond Modernity: Reflections of a Post-Modern Catholic.* San Francisco: Ignatius Press, 1987.

"St. Maximilian Kolbe: Priest Hero of a Death Camp." Catholic-Pages Web site. May 15, 2007. http://www.catholic-pages.com/saints/st_maximilian.asp.

Safire, William, comp. *Lend Me Your Ears: Great Speeches in History.* New York: W. W. Norton, 1992.

Schall, James V. *The Regensburg Lecture.* South Bend, IN: St. Augustine's Press, 2007.

Scharfenberg, Joachim. *Sigmund Freud and His Critique of Religion.* Translated by O. C. Dean, Jr. Philadelphia: Fortress, 1988.

Schlesinger, Arthur M., Jr. *The Disuniting of America: Reflections on a Multicultural Society.* Rev. ed. New York: W. W. Norton, 1998.

Schoenborn, Christopher. *With Jesus Every Day: How Believing Transforms Living.* Edited by Hubert Philipp Weber; translated by Brian McNeil. New York: Crossroad Pub. Co., 2006.

Scholem, Gershom. *Kabbalah.* New York: Dorset, 1987.

Schor, Juliet. *The Overspent American: Upscaling, Downshifting, and the New Consumer.* New York: Basic Books, 1998.

Scola, Angelo. *The Nuptial Mystery.* Translated by Michelle Borras. Grand Rapids: Eerdmans, 2005.

Shivanandan, Mary. *Crossing the Threshold of Love: A New Vision of Marriage in the Light of John Paul II's Anthropology.* Washington, D.C.: Catholic Univ. of America Press, 1999.

Silone, Ignazio. *Bread and Wine.* Translated by Harvey Fergusson II. New York: Signet, 1963.

Solovyov, Vladimir. *The Meaning of Love.* Translated by Thomas R. Beyer Jr. and Jane Marshall. West Stockbridge, MA: Lindisfarne, 1995.

Spiegelman, Art. *Maus: A Survivor's Tale* (New York: Pantheon, 1997), excerpted in Brunetti.

Stossel, Scott. *Sarge: The Life and Times of Sargent Shriver.* Washington, D.C.: Smithsonian Books, 2004.

Synod of Bishops. Special Assembly for America. "Encounter with the Living Jesus Christ: The Way to Conversion, Community and Solidarity in America." Lineamenta. Vatican City, January 12, 1997. General Secretariat of the Synod of Bishops and *Libreria Editrice Vaticana.* http://www.vatican.va/roman_curia/synod/documents/rc_synod_doc_01081996_usa-lineam_en.html.

Szulc, Tad. *Pope John Paul II: The Biography.* New York: Scribner, 1995.

Tarnas, Richard. *The Passion of the Western Mind: Understanding the Ideas That Have Shaped Our World View.* New York: Harmony, 1991.

Taylor, Charles. *Sources of the Self: The Making of the Modern Identity.* Cambridge: Harvard Univ. Press, 1989.

Teresa of Calcutta. *Mother Teresa: Come Be My Light: The Private Writings of the Saint of Calcutta.* Edited by Brian Kolodiejchuk. New York: Doubleday, 2007.

———. "Nobel Peace Prize Lecture." Nobel Peace Prize Award Ceremony. Oslo City Hall, Norway. December 11, 1979. Nobel

Foundation. http://nobelprize.org/nobel_prizes/peace/laureates/ 1979/teresa-lecture.html.

———. "Quotes from Mother Teresa." *USA Today, 1977.* http://www. usatoday.com/news/mothert/mother04.htm.

Terkel, Studs. *Working: People Talk about What They Do All Day and How They Feel about What They Do.* New York: Pantheon, 1974.

Thucydides. *History of the Peloponnesian War.* Translated by Charles Forster Smith. 4 vols. Rev. ed. Cambridge, MA: Loeb Classical Library, 1928.

Thomas Aquinas. *The Summa Theologica of St. Thomas Aquinas.* Second and Revised Edition, 1912-22. Translated by Fathers of the English Dominican Province. New York: Benziger, 1912-22. Online Edition by Kevin Knight, 2006. http://www.newadvent .org/summa/

Tischner, Józef. *The Spirit of Solidarity.* Translated by Marek B. Zaleski and Benjamin Fiore. San Francisco: Harper & Row, 1984.

Tocqueville, Alexis de. *Democracy in America.* Edited by J. P. Mayer. Translated by George Lawrence. Garden City, NY: Doubleday, 1969.

Tsu, Lao. *Tao Te Ching.* Translated by Gia-fu Feng and Jane English. New York: Vintage, 1972.

Twomey, D. Vincent. *Pope Benedict XVI: The Conscience of Our Age.* San Francisco: Ignatius Press, 2007.

United States Conference of Catholic Bishops. Hispanic Affairs Office. "Demographics." October 24, 2006. http://www.nccbuscc.org/hispanicaffairs/demo.shtml.

———. *Forming Consciences for Faithful Citizenship: A Call to Political Responsibility from the Catholic Bishops of the United States.* November 14, 2007. http://www.usccb.org/bishops/FCStatement.pdf.

Vanier, Jean. *Becoming Human.* Mahwah, NJ: Paulist Press, 1998.

———. *From Brokenness to Community.* New York: Paulist Press, 1992

von Balthasar, Hans Urs. *Love Alone Is Credible.* Translated by D. C. Schindler. San Francisco: Ignatius Press, 2004.

von Hildebrand, Alice. *The Privilege of Being a Woman.* Michigan: Veritas Press, 2002.

Vorgrimler, Herbert, ed. *Commentary on the Documents of Vatican 11.* Vol. 5. Translated by W. J. O'Hara. New York: Herder & Herder, 1969.

Waite, Linda, et al., "Does Divorce Make People Happy?: Findings from a Study of Unhappy Marriages." New York: Institute for American Values, 2002. http://www.americanvalues.org/html/does_divorce_make_people_happy.html.

Weaver, Richard. *Ideas Have Consequences.* Chicago: Univ. of Chicago Press, 1948.

Weigel, George. *God's Choice: Pope Benedict XVI and the Future of the Catholic Church.* New York: HarperCollins, 2005.

————. *Witness to Hope: The Biography of Pope John Paul II.* New York: HarperCollins, 1999.

Whitehead, Barbara Dafoe. *The Divorce Culture.* New York: Vintage Books, 1996.

Wiesel, Elie. *Night.* Translated by Marion Wiesel. New York: Hill & Wang, 2006.

Wolf, Naomi. "Our Bodies, Our Souls." *New Republic,* October 16, 1995, 26–35.

Yeats, William Butler. *The Collected Poems of W. B. Yeats.* 2nd ed. New York: Macmillan, 1956.

Zedillo, Ernesto. "Give Globalization a Hand." *Forbes,* October 2, 2006. http://www.forbes.com/columnists/forbes/2006/1002/027.html.